Getting Acquainted with the Trees

by J. Horace McFarland

Foreword

These sketches are, I fear, very unscientific and unsystematic. They record the growth of my own interest and information, as I have recently observed and enjoyed the trees among which I had walked unseeing far too many years. To pass on, as well as I can, some of the benefit that has come into my own life from this wakened interest in the trees provided by the Creator for the resting of tired brains and the healing of ruffled spirits, as well as for utility, is the reason for gathering together and somewhat extending the papers that have brought me, as they have appeared in the pages of "The Outlook," so many letters of fellowship and appreciation from others who have often seen more clearly and deeply into the woods than I may hope to.

Driven out from my desk by weariness sometimes--and as often, I confess, by a rasped temper I would fain hide from display--I have never failed to find rest, and peace, and much to see and to love, among the common and familiar trees, to which I hope these mere hints of some of their features not always seen may send others who also need their silent and beneficent message.

J. H. McF.

March 17, 1904

Contents

A Story of Some Maples

This is not a botanical disquisition; it is not a complete account of all the members of the important tree family of maples. I am not a botanist, nor a true scientific observer, but only a plain tree-lover, and I have been watching some trees bloom and bud and grow and fruit for a few years, using a camera now and then to record what I see--and much more than I see, usually!

In the sweet springtime, when the rising of the sap incites some to poetry, some to making maple sugar, and some to watching for the first flowers, it is well to look at a few tree-blooms, and to consider the possibilities and the pleasures of a peaceful hunt that can be made with profit in city street or park, as well as along country roadsides and in the meadows and the woods.

Who does not know of the maples that are all around us? Yet who has seen the commonest of them bloom in very early spring, or watched the course of the peculiar winged seed-pods or "keys" that follow the flowers? The white or "silver" maple of streets or roadsides, the soft maple of the woods, is one of the most familiar of American trees. Its rapid and vigorous growth endears it to the man who is in a hurry for shade, and its sturdy limbs are the joy of the tree-butcher who "trims" them short in later years.

Watch this maple in very early spring--even before spring is any more than a calendar probability--and a singular bloom will be found along the slender twigs. Like little loose-haired brushes these flowers are, coming often bravely in sleet and snow, and seemingly able to "set" and fertilize regardless of the weather. They hurry through the bloom-time, as they must do to carry out the life-round, for the graceful two-winged seeds that follow them are picked up and whirled about by April winds, and, if they lodge in the warming earth, are fully able to grow into fine little trees the same season. Examine these seed-pods, keys, or samaras (this last is a scientific name with such euphony to it that it might well become common!), and notice the delicate veining in the translucent wings. See the graceful lines of the whole thing, and realize what an abundant provision Dame Nature makes for reproduction,--for a moderate-sized tree completes many thousands of these finely formed, greenish yellow, winged samaras, and casts them loose for the wind to distribute during enough days to secure the best chances of the season.

This same silver maple is a bone of contention among tree-men, at times. Some will tell you it is "coarse"; and so it is when planted in an improper place upon a narrow street, allowed to flourish unrestrained for years, and then ruthlessly cropped off to a headless trunk! But set it on a broad lawn, or upon a roadside with generous room, and its noble stature and grace need yield nothing to the most artistic elm of New England. And in the deep woods it sometimes reaches a majesty and a dignity that compel admiration. The great maple at Eagles Mere is the king of the bit of primeval forest yet remaining to that mountain rest spot. It towers high over mature hemlocks and beeches, and seems well able to defy future centuries.

But there is another very early maple to watch for, and it is one widely distributed in the Eastern States. The red or scarlet maple is well named, for its flowers, not any more conspicuous in form than those of its close relation, the silver maple, are usually bright red or yellow, and they give a joyous color note in the very beginning of spring's overture. Not long are these flowers with us; they fade, only to be quickly succeeded by even more brilliant samaras, a little more delicate and refined than those of the silver maple, as well as of the richest and warmest hue. Particularly in New England does this maple provide a notable spring color showing.

The leaves of the red maple--it is also the swamp maple of some localities-- as they open to the coaxing of April sun and April showers, have a special charm. They are properly red, but mingled with the characteristic color is a whole palette of tints of soft yellow, bronze and apricot. As the little baby leaflets open, they are shiny and crinkly, and altogether attractive. One thinks of the more aristocratic and dwarfed Japanese maples, in looking at the opening of these red-brown beauties, and it is no pleasure to see them smooth out into sedate greenness. Again, in fall, a glory of color comes to the leaves of the red maple; for they illumine the countryside with their scarlet hue, and, as they drop, form a brilliant thread in the most beautiful of all carpets--that of the autumn leaves. I think no walk in the really happy days of the fall maturity of growing things is quite so pleasant as that which leads one to shuffle through this deep forest floor covering of oriental richness of hue.

As the ground warms and the sun searches into the hearts of the buds, the Norway maple, familiar street tree of Eastern cities, breaks into a wonderful bloom. Very deceptive it is, and taken for the opening foliage by the casual observer; yet there is, when these flowers first open, no hint of leaf on the tree, save that of the swelling bud. All that soft haze of greenish yellow is bloom, and bloom of the utmost beauty. The charm lies not in boldness of color or of contrast, but at the other extreme--in the delicacy of differing tints, in the variety of subtle shades and tones. There are charms of form and of fragrance, too, in this Norway maple--the flowers are many-rayed stars, and they emit a faint, spicy odor, noticeable only when several trees are together in bloom. And these flowers last long, comparatively; so long that the greenish yellow of the young leaves begins to combine with them before they fall. The tints of flower and of leaf melt insensibly into each other, so that, as I have remarked before, the casual observer says, "The leaves are out on the Norway maples,"--not knowing of the great mass of delightful flowers that have preceded the leaves above his unseeing eyes. I emphasize this, for I hope some of my readers may be on the outlook for a new pleasure in early spring--the blooming of this maple, with flowers so thoroughly distinct and so entirely beautiful.

The samaras to follow on this Norway maple are smaller than those of the other two maples mentioned, and they hang together at a different angle, somewhat more graceful. I have often wondered how the designers, who work to death the pansies, the roses and the violets, have managed to miss a form or "motive" of such value, suggesting at once the near-by street and far-away Egypt.

A purely American species, and one of as much economic importance as any leaf-dropping tree, is the sugar maple, known also as rock maple--one designation because we can get sweetness from its sap, the other because of the hardness of its wood. The sugar maples of New England, to me, are more individual and almost more essentially beautiful than the famed elms. No saccharine life-blood is drawn from the elm; therefore its elegance is considered. I notice that we seldom think much of beauty when it attaches to something we can eat! Who realizes that the common corn, the American maize, is a stately and elegant plant, far more beautiful than many a pampered pet of the greenhouse? But this is not a corn story--I shall hope to be heard on the neglected beauty of many common things, some day--and we can for the time overlook the syrup of the sugar maple for its delicate blossoms, coming long after the red and the silver are done with their flowers. These sugar-maple blooms hang on slender stems; they come with the first leaves, and are very different in appearance from the flowers of other maples. The observer will have no trouble in recognizing them after the first successful attempt, even though he may be baffled in comparing the maple leaves by the apparent similarity of the foliage of the Norway, the sugar and the sycamore maples at certain stages of growth.

After all, it is the autumn time that brings this maple most strongly before us, for it flaunts its banners of scarlet and yellow in the woods, along the roads, with an insouciant swing of its own. The sugar possibility is forgotten, and it is a pure autumn pleasure to appreciate the richness of color, to be soon followed by the more sober cognizance of the elegance of outline and form disclosed when all the delicate tracery of twig and bough stands revealed against winter's frosty sky. The sugar maple has a curious habit of ripening or reddening some of its branches very early, as if it was hanging out a warning signal to the squirrels and the chipmunks to hurry along with their storing of nuts against the winter's need. I remember being puzzled one August morning as I drove along one of Delaware's flat, flat roads, to know what could possibly have produced the brilliant, blazing scarlet banner that hung across a distant wood as if a dozen red flags were being there displayed. Closer approach disclosed one rakish branch on a sugar maple, all afire with color, while every other leaf on the tree yet held the green of summer.

Again in the mountains, one late summer, half a lusty sugar maple set up a conflagration which, I was informed, presaged its early death. But the next summer it grew as freely as ever, and retained its sober green until the cool days and nights; just as if the ebullition of the season previous was but a breaking out of extra color life, rather than a suggestion of weakness or death.

The Norway maple is botanically Acer platanoides, really meaning plane-like maple, from the similarity of its leaves to those of the European plane. The sycamore maple is Acer Pseudo-platanus, which, being translated, means that old Linneus thought it a sort of false plane-like maple. Both are European species, but both are far more familiar, as street and lawn trees, to us dwellers in cities than are many of our purely American species. There is a little difference in the bark of the two, and the leaves of the sycamore, while almost identical in form, are darker and thicker than those of the Norway, and they are whitish underneath, instead of light green. The habit of the two is twin-like; they can scarcely be distinguished when the leaves are off. But the flowers are totally different, and one would hardly believe them to be akin, judging only by appearances. The young leaves of the sycamore maple are lush and vigorous when the long, grape-like flower-clusters appear below the twigs. "Racemes" they are, botanically--and that is another truly good scientific word--while the beautiful Norway maple's flowers must stand the angular designation of "corymbs." But don't miss looking for the sycamore maple's long, pendulous racemes. They seem more grape-like than grape blossoms; and they stay long, apparently, the transition from flower to fruit being very gradual. I mind me of a sycamore I pass every winter day, with its dead fruit-clusters, a reminiscence of the flower-racemes, swinging in the frosty breeze, waiting until the spring push of the life within the twigs shoves them off.

To be ready to recognize this maple at the right time, it is well to observe and mark the difference between it and the Norway in the summer time, noting the leaves and the bark as suggested above.

Another maple that is different is one variously known as box-elder, ash-leaved maple, or negundo. Of rapid growth, it makes a lusty, irregular tree. Its green-barked, withe-like limbs seem willing to grow in any direction--down, up, sidewise--and the result is a peculiar formlessness that has its own merit. I think of a fringe of box-elders along Paxton Creek, decked in early spring with true maple flowers on thread-like stems, each cluster surmounted by soft green foliage apparently borrowed from the ash, and it seems that no other tree could fit better into the place or the season. Then I remember another, a single stately tree that has had a great field all to itself, and stands up in superb dignity, dominating even the group of pin-oaks nearest to it. 'Twas the surprising mist of bloom on this tree that took me up the field on a run, one spring day, when the running was sweet in the air, but sticky underfoot. The color effect of the flowers is most delicate, and almost indescribable in ordinary chromatic terms. Don't miss the acquaintance of the ash-leaved maple at its flowering time, in the very flush of the springtime, my tree-loving friends!

I have not found a noticeable fragrance in the flowers of the box-elder, such as is very apparent where there is a group of Norway maples in bloom together. The red maples also give to the air a faint and delightfully spicy odor, under favorable conditions. May I hint that the lusty box-elder, when it is booming along its spring growth, furnishes a loose-barked whistle stick about as good as those that come from the willow? The generous growth that provides its loosening sap can also spare a few twigs for the boys, and they will be all the better for a melodious reason for the spring ramble.

The striped maple of Pennsylvania, a comparatively rare and entirely curious small tree or large shrub, is not well known, though growing freely as "elkwood" and "moosewood" in the Alleghanies, because it is rather hard to transplant, and thus offers no inducements to the nurserymen. These good people, like the rest of us, move along the lines of least resistance, wherefore many a fine tree or fruit is rare to us, because shy or difficult of growth, or perhaps unsymmetrical. The fine Rhode Island Greening apple is unpopular because the young tree is crooked, while the leather-skinned and punk-fleshed Ben Davis is a model of symmetry and rapidity of growth. Our glorious tulip tree of the woods, because of its relative difficulty in transplanting, has had to be insisted upon from the nurserymen by those who know its superb beauty. For the same reason this small charming maple, with the large, soft, comfortable leaves upon which the deer love to browse, is kept from showing its delicate June bloom and its remarkable longitudinally striped bark in our home grounds. I hope some maple friends will look for it, and, finding, admire this, the aristocrat among our native species.

The mountain maple--the nurserymen call it Acer spicatum--is another native of rather dwarf growth. It is bushy, and not remarkable in leaf, its claim for distinction being in its flowers and samaras, which are held saucily up, above the branches on which they grow, rather than drooping modestly, as other maples gracefully bear their bloom and fruit. These shiny seeds or keys are brightly scarlet, as well, and thus very attractive in color. There is a reason for this, in nature's economy; for while the loosely hung samaras of the other maples are distributed by the breezes, the red pods of this mountain maple hold stiffly upward to attract the birds upon whom it largely depends for that sowing which must precede its reproduction.

Of the other maples of America--a score of them there are--I might write pages, to weariness. The black maple of the Eastern woods, the large-leaved maples of the West, these and many more are in this great family, to say nothing of the many interesting cultivated forms and variations introduced from European nurseries, and most serviceable in formal ornamental planting.

But I have told of those I know best and those that any reader can know as well in one season, if he looks for them with the necessary tree love which is but a fine form of true love of God's creation. This love, once implanted, means surer protection for the trees, otherwise so defenseless against the unthinking vandalism of commercialism or incompetence--a vandalism that has not only devastated our American forests, but mutilated shamefully many trees of priceless value in and about our cities.

Of the Japanese maples--their leaves seemingly a showing of the ingenuity of these Yankees of the Orient, in their twists of form and depths of odd color--I could tell a tale, but it would be of the tree nursery and not of the broad outdoors. Let us close the book and go afield, in park or meadow, on street or lawn, and look to the maples for an unsuspected feast of bloom, if it be spring, or for richness of foliage in summer and autumn; and in coldest winter let us notice the delicate twigs and yet sturdy structure of this tree family that is most of all characteristic of the home, in city or country.

The Growth of the Oak

The old saw has it, "Great oaks from little acorns grow," and all of us who remember the saying have thus some idea of what the beginning of an oak is. But what of the beginning of the acorn? In a general way, one inferentially supposes that there must be a flower somewhere in the life-history of the towering white oak that has defied the storms of centuries and seems a type of everything sturdy and strong and masculine; but what sort of a flower could one imagine as the source of so much majesty? We know of the great magnolias, with blooms befitting the richness of the foliage that follows them. We see, and some of us admire, the exquisitely delicate blossoms of that splendid American tree, the tulip or whitewood. We inhale with delight the fragrance that makes notable the time when the common locust sends forth its white racemes of loveliness. But we miss, many of us, the flowering of the oaks in early spring, and we do not realize that this family of trees, most notable for rugged strength, has its bloom of beginning at the other end of the scale, in flowers of delicate coloring and rather diminutive size.

The reason I missed appreciating the flowers of the oak--they are quite new to me--for some years of tree admiration was because of the distracting accompaniment the tree gives to the blooms. Some trees--most of the maples, for instance--send out their flowers boldly ahead of the foliage, and it is thus easy to see what is happening above your head, as you stroll along drinking in the spring's nectar of spicy air. Others, again, have such showy blooms that the mass of foliage only accentuates their attractiveness, and it is not possible to miss them.

But the oak is different; it is, as modest as it is strong, and its bloom is nearly surrounded by the opening leaves in most seasons and in most of the species I am just beginning to be acquainted with. Then, too, these opening leaves are of such indescribable colors--if the delicate chromatic tints they reflect to the eye may be so strongly named--that they harmonize, and do not contrast, with the flowers. It is with them almost as with a fearless chipmunk whose acquaintance I cultivated one summer--he was gay with stripes of soft color, yet he so fitted any surroundings he chose to be in that when he was quiet he simply disappeared! The oak's flowers and its exquisite unfolding of young foliage combine in one effect, and it is an effect so beautiful that one easily fails to separate its parts, or to see which of the mass of soft pink, gray, yellow and green is bloom and which of it is leafage.

Take the pin-oak, for instance, and note the softness of the greenery above its flowers. Hardly can we define the young leaves as green--they are all tints, and all beautiful. This same pin-oak, by the way (I mean the one the botanists call Quercus palustris), is a notable contradiction of the accepted theory that an oak of size and dignity cannot be reared in a lifetime. There are hundreds of lusty pin-oaks all over the Eastern States that are shading the homes of the wise men who planted them in youth, and they might well adorn our parks and avenues in place of many far less beautiful and permanent trees. With ordinary care, and in good soil, the pin-oak grows rapidly, and the characteristic spreading habit and the slightly down-drooping branches are always attractive. In its age it has not the ruggedness of its kin, though it assumes a stately and somewhat formal habit, and, I must confess, accumulates some ragged dead branches in its interior.

This raggedness is easily cared for, for the tree requires--and few trees do-- no "trimming" of its outer branches. The interior twigs that the rapid growth of the tree has deprived of air and light can be quickly and easily removed. In Washington, where street-tree planting has been and is intelligently managed under central authority, the avenues of pin-oaks are a splendid feature of the great boulevards which are serving already as a model to the whole country. Let us plant oaks, and relieve the monotony of too many maples, poplars and horse-chestnuts along our city and village highways.

I like, too, to see the smooth little acorns of the pin-oak before the leaves drop; they seem so finished and altogether pleasing, and with the leaves make a classical decorative motive worth more attention from designers.

While I am innocent of either ability or intent to write botanically of the great oak family, I ought perhaps to transcribe the information that the flowers we see--if we look just at the right time in the spring--are known as "staminate catkins,"--which, being interpreted, means that there are also pistillate flowers, much less conspicuous, but exceedingly necessary if acorns are to result; and also the fact that the familiar "pussy-willow" of our acquaintance is the same form of bloom--the catkin, or ament. I ought to say, too, that some of the oaks perfect acorns from blossoms in one year, while others must grow through two seasons before they are mature. Botanically, the oak family is nearly a world family, and we Americans, though possessed of many species, have no monopoly of it. Indeed, if I may dare to refer the reader to that great storehouse of words, the Encyclop鎆ia Britannica, I think he will find that the oak is there very British, and that the English oak, surely a magnificent tree in England anyway, is patriotically glorified to the writer.

But we want to talk of some of our own oaks. The one thoroughly characteristic is surely the noble white oak, a tree most admirable in every way, and most widely distributed over the Northern States. Its majestic form, as it towers high above the ordinary works of man, conveys the repose of conscious strength to the beholder. There is a great oak in Connecticut to which I make pilgrimages, and from which I always get a message of rest and peace. There it stands, strong, full-powered, minding little the most furious storms, a benediction to every one who will but lift his eyes. There it has stood in full majesty for years unknown, for it was a great oak, so run the title-deeds, way back in 1636, when first the white man began to own land in the Connecticut Valley. At first sight it seems not large, for its perfect symmetry conceals its great size; but its impression grows as one looks at it, until it seems to fill the whole landscape. I have sat under it in spring, when yet its leafy canopy was incomplete; I have looked into its green depths in midsummer, when its grateful shadow refreshed the highway; I have seen the sun set in redness beyond its bare limbs, the snowy countryside emphasizing its noble lines; I have tried to fathom the mystery in its sturdy heart overhead when the full moon rode in the sky; and always that "great oak of Glastonbury" has soothed and cheered and rested, and taken me nearer the Giver of all such good to restless humanity.

Do I wonder at my friend who has built his home where he may look always at this white oak, or that he raged in anger when a crabbed neighbor ruthlessly cut down a superb tree of the same kind that was on his property line, in order that he might run his barbed-wire fence straight? No; I agree with him that this tree-murderer has probably a barbed-wire heart, and we expect that his future existence will be treeless, at least!

Sometimes this same white oak adapts itself to the bank of a stream, though its true character develops best in the drier ground. Its strength has been its bane, for the value of its timber has caused many a great isolated specimen to be cut down. It is fine to know that some States--Massachusetts, Connecticut, and Rhode Island also, I think--have given to trees along highways, and in situations where they are part of the highway landscape, the protection of a wise law. Under this law each town appoints a tree-warden, serving without pay (and therefore with love), who may seal to the town by his label such trees as are truly the common possession, regardless of whose land they happen to be on. If the owner desires to cut down a tree thus designated, he must first obtain permission, after stating satisfactory reasons, of the annual town-meeting, and this is not so easy as to make cutting very frequent. The whole country should have such a law, and I should enjoy its application right here in Pennsylvania, where oaks of a hundred years have been cut down to make room for a whisky sign, and where a superb pin-oak that I passed today is devoted to an ignominious use. If I may venture to become hortatory, let me say that the responsibility for the preservation of the all-too-few remaining great primeval trees, and of their often notable progeny, in our Eastern States, rests with those who care for trees, not alone with those who ought to care. To talk about the greatness and beauty of a fine oak or maple or tulip, to call attention to its shade value, and to appeal to the cupidity of the ground owner by estimating how much less his property will be worth when the trees are gone or have been mishandled, will aid to create the necessary public sentiment. And to provide wise laws, as may be often done with proper attention, is the plain duty and the high privilege of the tree-loving citizen. The trees are defenseless, and they are often unreplaceable; if you love them protect them as you would your children.

The white-oak leaf is the most familiar and characteristic, perhaps, of the family; but other species, close to the white oak in habit, show foliage of a very different appearance. The swamp white oak, for instance, is a noble tree, and in winter particularly its irregular branches give it an especial expression of rugged strength as it grows along a brookside; but its leaves smooth up on the edges, giving only a hint of the deep serrations that typify its upland brother. Deeply green above are these leaves and softly white below, and in late summer there appears, here and there, on a stout stem, a most attractive acorn of large size. Its curious cup gives a hint, or more than a hint, as to the special designating character of another oak, the mossy-cup or bur. This latter species is beautiful in its habit, rich in its foliage, and the fringed or mossed acorns are of a remarkable size.

[Illustration: An old post-oak]

Of all the oaks, the sturdy but not lofty post-oak spreads the richest display of foliage. Its peculiar habit leads to the even placing of its violoncello-shaped leaves, and its generous crop of acorns gives added distinction in late summer. It is fine in the forest, and a notable ornament anywhere.

It has been said that a proper penance for an offending botanist would be a compulsory separation and description of the involved and complicated goldenrod family; and I would suggest that a second edition of the same penance might be a requirement to name off-hand the first dozen oak trees the same poor botanist might meet. So much do the foliage, the bark, and the habit of growth vary, and so considerable is the difference between individuals of the same species, that the wisest expert is likely to be the most conservative. An unbotanical observer, who comes at the family just because he loves trees in general, and is poking his eyes and his camera into unusual places, doesn't make close determinations; he tells what he thinks he sees, and leaves exact work to the scientists.

There are some oaks, however, that have borrowed the foliage of other trees so cunningly that one at first scouts the possibility of the Quercus parentage, until he sees an undeniable acorn thrusting itself forward. Then he is sure that what seemed a rather peculiarly shaped chestnut tree, with somewhat stumpy foliage, is none other than the chestnut-oak. A fine tree it is, too, this same chestnut-oak, with its masquerading foliage of deep green, its upright and substantial habit, its rather long and aristocratic-looking acorns. The authorities tell that its wood, too, is brownish and valuable; but we tree-lovers are not enthusiastic over mere timber values, because that means the killing of the trees.

The willow-oak will not deceive, because its habit is so oak-like and so willow-less; but its foliage is surely borrowed from its graceful and more rapidly growing neighbor. Not so large, by any means, as the white oak or the chestnut-oak, it has somewhat rough and reddish bark, and its acorns are perfected in the second year of their growth, close to the twigs, in the way of the pin-oak. The general aspect of the tree is upright, rather than spreading, and it partakes thus of the maple character in its landscape effect. The willow-oak is one of the species I would, if I were writing a tree-planting article, heartily commend to those who wish to add adornment to the countryside that shall be permanent and satisfactory. Just a hint here: nursery-grown oaks, now obtainable from any modern establishment, have usually been frequently moved or transplanted, as the trade term goes, and this means that they have established a somewhat self-contained root system, which will give them far greater vigor and cause them to take hold sooner when finally placed in a situation where they are to be permanent features. The reason is plain: the forest seedling, in the fierce struggle for existence usually prevailing, must send its roots far and wide for food, and when it is dug out their feeding capacity is so seriously curtailed as to check the growth of the tree for many years. The nursery-grown tree, on the contrary, has been brought up "by hand," and its food has always been convenient to it, leading to more rapid growth and a more compact root system. I only interject this prosaic fact here in the hope that some of my tree-loving readers will undertake to plant some oaks instead of only the soft-wooded and less permanent maples, poplars, and the like.

Another simulative leaf is that of the laurel-oak, and it is color and gloss as well as shape that have been borrowed from its humbler neighbor in the forest. The shining green of the laurel is seen in these oak leaves; they are also half evergreen, thus being one of the family particularly belonging to our Southern States, and hardly enduring the chill of the winters north of Virginia. It is one of the galaxy of oaks I remember as providing a special interest in the Georgia forests, where the long-leaved pine also gave a new tree sensation to the visitor from the North, who at first could hardly imagine what those lovely little green fountains of foliage were that he saw along the roadside and in the woods. The Georgia oaks seem to me to have a richness of foliage, a color and substance and shine, that compare only with the excellence of two other products of the same State--the peach and the watermelon. The long summer and the plenitude of sunshine seem to weave into these products luxuriance found nowhere else; and when one sees for the first time a happy, rollicking bunch of round-eyed negro children, innocent alike of much clothing or any trouble, mixing up with the juicy Georgia melon under the shade of a luxuriant oak, he gets a new conception of at least one part of the race problem!

One of the things I wanted much to see when I first traveled South was the famed live-oak, the majesty and the mournfulness of which had been long sung into me. Perhaps I expected too much, as I did of the palmetto, another part of my quest, but surely there was disappointment when I was led, on the banks of the Manatee River in Florida, to see a famous live-oak. It was tall and grand, but its adornment of long, trailing gray Spanish moss, which was to have attached the sadness to it, seemed merely to make it unkempt and uncomfortable. I was instantly reminded of a tree at home in the far North that I had never thought particularly beautiful, but which now, by comparison, took on an attractiveness it has never since lost. Imagine a great spreading weeping willow turned dingy gray, and you have a fair picture of a moss-covered live-oak; but you will prefer it green, as is the willow, I believe.

One day a walk about Savannah, which city has many splendid live-oaks in its parks and squares, involved me in a sudden shower, when, presto! the weeping willow of the North was reincarnated before my eyes, for the falling rain turned the dingy moss pendants of the live-oak to the whitish green that makes the willow such a delightful color-note in early spring. I have been thankful often for that shower, for it gave a better feeling about the live-oak, and made me admire the weeping willow.

The live-oak, by the way, has a leaf very little like the typical oak--it is elliptical in shape and smooth in outline. The curious parasitic moss that so frequently covers the tree obscures the really handsome foliage.

The English Oak, grand tree that it is, grows well in America, as everything English should by right, and there are fine trees of this Quercus Robur on Long Island. The acorns are of unusual elegance, as the photograph which shows them will prove.

The red oak, the black oak, the scarlet oak, all splendid forest trees of the Northeast, are in the group of confusion that can be readily separated only by the timber-cruiser, who knows every tree in the forest for its economic value, or by the botanist, with his limp-bound Gray's Manual in hand. I confess to bewilderment in five minutes after the differences have been explained to me, and I enjoyed, not long ago, the confusion of a skilful nurseryman who was endeavoring to show me his young trees of red oak which the label proved to be scarlet! But the splendidly effective trees themselves can be fully appreciated, and the distinctions will appear as one studies carefully the features of these living gifts of nature's greenness. The trees wait on one, and once the habit of appreciation and investigation is formed, each walk afield, in forest or park, leads to the acquirement of some new bit of tree-lore, that becomes more precious and delightful as it is passed on and commented upon in association with some other member of the happily growing fraternity of nature-lovers.

[Illustration: Acorns of the English oak]

These oak notes are not intended to be complete, but only to suggest some points for investigation and appreciation to my fellows in the brotherhood. I have never walked between Trenton and New York, and therefore never made the desired acquaintance with the scrub-oaks along the way. Nor have I dipped as fully into the oak treasures of the Arnold Arboretum as I want to some day. But my camera is yet available and the trees are waiting; the tree love is growing and the tree friends are inviting, and together we will add to the oak knowledge and to that thankfulness for God and life and love and friends that the trees do most constantly cause to flourish.

The Pines

In popular estimation, the pines seem to belong to the North, not quite so exclusively as do the palms to the South. The ragged, picturesque old pines, spruces and hemlocks of our remembrance carry with them the thought of great endurance, long life and snowy forests. We think of them, too, as belonging to the mountains, not to the plains; as clothing steep slopes with their varied deep greens rather than as standing against the sky-line of the sea. Yet I venture to think that the most of us in the East see oftenest the pines peculiar to the lowlands, as we flit from city to city over the steel highways of travel, and have most to do, in an economical sense, with a pine that does not come north of the Carolinas--the yellow pine which furnishes our familiar house-flooring.

The pine family, as we discuss it, is not all pines, in exactitude--it includes many diverse trees that the botanist describes as conifers. These cone-bearing trees are nearly all evergreens--that is, the foliage persists the year round, instead of being deciduous, as the leaf-dropping maples, oaks, birches, and the like are scientifically designated. Historically the pines are of hoary age, for they are closely related to the growths that furnished the geologic coal measures stored up in the foundations of the earth for our use now. Economically, too, all the pine family together is of vast importance--"the most important order of forest trees in the economy of civilized man," says Dr. Fernow; for, as he adds, the cone-bearing trees "have furnished the bulk of the material of which our civilization is built." As usual, civilization has destroyed ruthlessly, thoughtlessly, almost viciously, in using this material; wherefore the devastation of the forests, moving them back from us farther and farther until in many regions they are but a thin fringe, has left most of us totally unfamiliar with these trees, of the utmost beauty as well as of the greatest value.

To know anything at all of the spruces, pines and hemlocks is to love them for the refreshment there is in their living presence, rather than to consider them merely for the timber value. But the point of view differs immensely with one's occupation. I remember finding in the depths of an Alleghany forest a comparatively rare native orchid, then new to me--the round-leaved or orbicular habenaria. While I was gloating over it with my camera a gray-haired native of the neighborhood joined me, and, to my surprise, assisted in the gloating--he, too, loved the woods and the plants. Coming a little later to a group of magnificent hemlocks, with great, clean, towering trunks reaching up a hundred feet through the soft maples and yellow birches and beeches which seemed dwarfed by these veterans, I exclaimed in admiration. "Yes," he said, "them's mighty fine hemlocks. I calc'late thet one to the left would bark near five dollars' wuth!" On the rare plant we had joined in esthetic appreciation, but the hemlock was to the old lumberman but a source of tan-bark.

This search for tannin, by the way, is to blame for much wanton destruction. Young hemlocks, from four to six inches in diameter, are felled, stripped of their bark, and left cumbering the ground, to invite fire and to make of the woods an unkempt cemetery. The fall of a tree from natural causes is followed by the interesting and beauty-making process of its mossy decay and return to the forest floor, furnishing in the process nourishment for countless seedlings and plants. A tree felled in maturity under enlightened forest management is all removed for its timber, and leaves the ground clear; but the operations of the bark-hunter leave only hideous destruction and a "slash" that is most difficult to clear in later years.

This same hemlock makes a most impressive forest. To walk among primeval hemlocks brings healing to the mind and peace to the soul, as one realizes fully that "the groves were God's first temples," and that God is close to one in these beneficent solitudes, where petty things must fall away, vexations cease, and man's spiritual nature absorb the message of the forest.

I wonder how many of my readers realize that an exquisite bit of real hemlock forest lies not five miles from Boston Common? At the Arnold Arboretum, that noble collection of trees and plants, "Hemlock Hill" is assuming deeper majesty year after year as its trees gain age and size. It presents exactly the pure forest conditions, and makes accessible to thousands the full beauty and soothing that nothing but a coniferous forest can provide for man. There is the great collateral advantage, too, that to reach Hemlock Hill, the visitor must use a noble entrance, and pass other trees and plants which, in the adequate setting here given, cannot but do him much good, and prepare him for the deep sylvan temple of the hemlocks he is seeking. To visit the Arboretum at the time when the curious variety of the apple relatives--pyruses and the like--bloom, is to secure a great benefit of sight and scent, and it is almost certain to make one resolve to return when these blossoms shall, by nature's perfect work, have become fruit. Here the fruit is grown for its beauty only, and thus no gastronomic possibilities interfere with the appreciation of color, and form, and situation! But again, to come to the Arboretum some time during the reign of the lilacs is to experience an even greater pleasure, perhaps, for here the old farm garden "laylock" assumes a wonderful diversity of form and color, from the palest wands of the Persian sorts to the deepest blue of some of the French hybrids.

The pines themselves will well repay any investigation and appreciation. Seven species are with us in the New England and Middle Atlantic States, seven more are found South, while the great West, with its yet magnificent forests, has twenty-five pines of distinct character. The white pine is perhaps most familiar to us, because of its economic importance, and it is as well the tallest and most notable of all those we see in the East. From its first essay as a seedling, with its original cluster of five delicate blue-green leaflets, to its lusty youth, when it is spreading and broad, if given room to grow, it is a fine object, and I have had some thrills of joy at finding this splendid common thing planted in well-placed groups on the grounds of wealthy men, instead of some Japanese upstart with a name a yard long and a truly crooked Oriental disposition! In age the white pine dominates any landscape, wearing even the scars of its long battle with the elements with stately dignity. A noble pair of white pines on the shore of Lake Champlain I remember especially--they were the monarchs of the lakeside as they towered above all other trees. Ragged they were, their symmetry gone long years ago through attacks of storms and through strife with the neighboring trees that had succumbed while they only suffered and stood firm. Yet they seemed all complete, of proved strength and staying power, and their aspect was not of defiance or anger, but rather indicative of beneficent strength, as if they said, "Here we stand; somewhat crippled, it is true, but yet pointing upright to the heavens, yet vigorous, yet seed-bearing and cheerful!"

Another group of these white pines that stood close to some only less picturesque red pines on the shores of a pond deep in the Adirondacks emphasized again for me one May day the majesty of this beneficent friend of mankind; and yet another old pine monarch against the sunset sky pointed the westward way from the picturesque Cornell campus, and alas! also pointed the danger to even this one unreplaceable tree when modern "enterprise" constructs a trolley line on a scenic route, ruthlessly destroying the very features that make the route desirable, rather than go to any mechanical trouble!

My readers will easily recall for themselves just the same sort of "old pine" groups they have record of on memory's picture-gallery, and will, I am sure, agree with me as to the informality, dignity and true beauty of these survivors of the forest, all of which deserve to be appreciatively cared for, against any encroachment of train, trolley or lumberman.

I am ashamed to say I have not yet seen the blossoms of the white pine, which the botanists tell us come in early spring, minute and light brown, to be followed by the six-inch-long cones which mature the second year. I promise my camera that another spring it shall be turned toward these shy blossoms.

Any one who has traveled south of Virginia, even by the Pullman way of not seeing, cannot fail to have noted the lovely green leaf-fountains springing up from the ground along the railroads. These are the young trees of the long-leaved or Southern yellow pine. How beautiful they are, these narrow leaves of vivid green, more than a foot long, drooping gracefully from the center outward, with none of the stiffness of our Northern species! In some places they seem to fairly bubble in green from all the surface of the ground, so close are they. And the grand long-leaved pine itself, maintained in lusty vigor above these greeneries, is a tree of simple dignity, emphasized strongly when seen at its best either in the uncut forest, or in a planted avenue. We of the North are helping to ruin the next generation of Southern pines by lavish use, for decorations, of the young trees of about two feet high, crowded with the long drooping emerald needles. The little cut-off pine lasts a week or two, in a parlor--it took four or five years to grow!

All pine-cones are interesting, and there is a great variation between the different species. The scrub-pine one sees along the railroads between New York and Philadelphia has rather stubby cones, while the pitch-pine, beloved of the fireplace for its "light-knots," has a somewhat pear-shaped and gracefully disposed cone. A most peculiar cone is that of a variety of the Norway pine, which, among other species brought from Europe, is valued for ornament. The common jack-pine of the Middle States hillsides wears symmetrical and handsome cones with dignity. Cones are, of course, the fruits or seed-holders of the pine, but the seeds themselves are found at the base of the scales, or parts of the cones, attached in pairs. Each cone, like an apple, has in its care a number of seeds, which it guards against various dangers until a kindly soil encourages the rather slow germination characteristic of the order.

The nurserymen have imported many pines from Europe, which give pleasing variety to our ornamental plantings, and aid in enriching the winter coloring. The Austrian pine and the Scotch pine are welcome additions to our own pine family. In these days of economic chemistry and a deficient rag supply, every reader of these words is probably in close proximity to an important spruce product--paper. The manufacturers say, with hand on heart, that they do not use much wood pulp, but when one has passed a great paper-mill flanked on all sides by piles of spruce logs, with no bales of rags in sight anywhere, he is tempted to think otherwise! Modern forestry is now planting trees on waste lands for the pulp "crop," and the common poplar is coming in to relieve the spruces.

Beautiful trees are these spruces and firs, either in the forest or when brought by the planter to his home grounds. The leaves are much shorter than those of most pines, and clothe the twigs closely. There is a vast variety in color, too, from the wonderful whitish or "glaucous" blue of the Colorado blue spruce, to the deep shining green of Nordmann's fir, a splendid introduction from the Caucasus. Look at them, glistening in the winter sun, or drooping with the clinging snow; walk in a spruce wood, inhaling the bracing balsamic fragrance which seems so kindly to the lungs; hark to the music of the wind in their tops, telling of health and purity, of God's love and provision for man's mind and heart, and you will begin to know the song of the firs. To really hear this grand symphony, for such it then becomes, you must listen to the wind playing on the tops of a great primeval coniferous forest, of scores and hundreds of acres or miles in extent. And even then, many visits are needed, for there are movements to this symphony--the allegro of the gale, the scherzo of the easy morning breeze, the deep adagio of a rain-storm, and the andante of warm days and summer breezes, when you may repose prone upon a soft carpet of pine needles, every sense made alert, yet soothed, by the master-theme you are hearing.

There is a little wood of thick young pines, interspersed with hard maple and an occasional birch, close by the lake of the Eagles, where my summers are made happy. The closeness of the pines has caused their lower branches to die, as always in the deep forest, and the falling needles, year by year, have deepened the soft brown carpet that covers the forest floor. Some one, years ago, struck by the aisles that the straight trunks mark out so clearly, called this the "Cathedral Woods." The name seems appropriate at all times, but especially when, on a warm Sunday afternoon, I lie at ease on the aromatic carpet, hearing the soft organ tones in the pine tops, and drinking in God's forest message.

I have visited these pine woods at midnight, when a full moon, making brilliant the near-by lake, gave but a ghostly gloom in the deep, deep silence of the Cathedral; but, more impressive, I have often trodden through in a white fog, when the distance was misty and dim, and the aisles seemed longer and higher, and to lead one further away from the trifles of temper and trial. Indeed, I do not believe that any one who has but once fully received from the deep forest that which it gives out so freely and constantly can ever think of things trivial, or of minor annoyances, while again within its soothing portals.

But of the trees of the forest of pine and spruce it must be noted that sometimes the deepest, glossiest green of the leaves as presented to the eye only hides the dainty, white-lined interior surface of those same leaves. To the outside, a somber dignity, unassailable, untouched by frost or sun, protective, defenseful, as nature often appears to the careless observer; but inside is light, softly reflected, revealing unsuspected delicacies of structure and finish.

To us who are not woodsmen or "timber-cruisers" the most familiar of all the spruces is the introduced form from Norway. Its yellowish green twigs are bright and cheerful, and in specimens that have reached the fruiting age the crown of cones, high up in the tree, is an additional charm, for these soft brown "strobiles," as the botanist calls them, are smooth and regular, and very different from those of the rugged pines. I have often been told that the Norway spruce was short-lived, and that it became unkempt in age; but now that I have lived for ten years and more beside a noble specimen, I know that the change from the upreaching push of youth to the semi-drooping sedateness of maturity is only a taking on of dignity. There stands on the home grounds of a true tree-lover in Pennsylvania a Norway spruce that has been untouched by knife or disaster since its planting many years ago. No pruning has shortened in its "leader" or top, no foolish idea of "trimming it up" has been allowed to deprive it of the very lowest branches, which, in consequence, now sweep the ground in full perfection, while the unchecked point of the tree still aspires upward forty feet above. A beautiful object is this tree--perhaps the most beautiful of all the conifers in my friend's great "pinetum," with its scores of rare species. Let me ask, then, those who would set this or any other tree of evergreen about the home, to see to it that the young tree from the nursery has all its lower branches intact, and that its top has never been mutilated. With care, such specimens may be obtained and successfully transplanted, and will grow in time to a lovely old age of steady greenness.

The balsam fir is almost indistinguishable from the Norway spruce when young, but soon grows apart from it in habit, and is hardly as desirable, even though a native. It is rich in the true balsamic odor; and this, again, is its destruction; for one "spruce pillow" may destroy a half dozen trees!

The white cedar, our common juniper, with its aromatic blue berries or fruits, is perhaps the most familiar of all the native evergreens. It comes to us of Pennsylvania all too freely at Christmas time, when the tree of joy and gifts may mean, in the wholesale, sad forest destruction. This juniper I have associated particularly with the dogwood and the red-bud, to the bloom of which it supplies a most perfect background in the favorite Conewago park, a purely natural reservation of things beautiful along the Pennsylvania railroad. Its lead-pencil sister, the red cedar, reaches our literary senses as closely as does the pulp-making spruce!

I might write much of the rare introduced cypresses from Japan and China, and of the peculiar variations that have been worked out by the nurserymen among the native pines and firs; yet this would not be talk of the trees of the open ground, but rather of the nursery and the park. Also, if I had but seen them, there would be much to say about the magnificent conifers of the great West, from the giant red-woods, or sequoias, of the Mariposa grove in California to the richly varied pines of the Rockies. But I can only suggest to my readers the intimate consideration of all this great pine family, so peculiarly valuable to mankind, and the use of some of the pines and spruces about the home for the steady cheer of green they so fully provide.

Apples

Well do I remember one of the admonitions of my youth, brought upon me by an attempt to take apple-blossoms from a tree in bloom because they were beautiful. I was told that it was wrong to pluck for any purpose the flowers of fruit trees, because the possible fruitage might thereby be reduced. That is, feeding the eye was improper, but it was always in order to conserve all the possibilities for another organ of the body. In those days we had not learned that nature provides against contingencies, and that not one-tenth of all the blossoms would be needed to "set" as much fruit as the tree could possibly mature.

The apple, well called the king of fruits, is worthy of all admiration as a fruit; but I do not see why that need interfere in the least with its consideration as an object of beauty. On the contrary, such consideration is all the better for the apple, which is not only most desirable and pleasing in its relation to the dessert, the truly celebrated American pie, the luscious dumpling of the housewife, and the Italian's fruit-stand of our cities, but is at the same time a benefaction to the eye and the sense of beauty, in tree, in blossom, and in fruit.

It is of the esthetic value of the apple I would write, leaving its supreme place in pomology unassailed. Look at the young apple tree in the "nursery row," where it has been growing a year since it was "budded"--that is, mysteriously changed from the wild and untamed fruit of nature to the special variety designed by the nurseryman. It is a straight, shapely wand, in most varieties, though it is curious to find that some apples, notably the favorite Rhode Island Greening, start in promptly to be picturesquely crooked and twisty. As it grows and branches under the cultivation and guidance of the orchardist, it maintains a lusty, hearty aspect, its yellowish, reddish or brownish twigs--again according to variety--spreading out to the sun and the air freely. A decade passes, and the sparse showing of bloom that has decorated it each spring gradually gives place to a great glory of flowers. The tree is about to bear, and it assumes the character of maturity; for while it grows on soberly for many years, there is now a spreading, a sort of relaxation, very different from the vigorous upshooting of its early youth. After a crop or two, the tree has become, to the eye, the familiar orchard member, and it leans a little from the blasts of winter, twists aside from the perpendicular, spreads comfortably over a great expanse of ground, and settles down to its long, useful, and truly beautiful life.

While the young orchard is trim and handsome, I confess to a greater liking for the rugged old trees that have followed blossom with fruit in unstinted profusion for a generation. There is a certain character of sturdy good-will about these substantial stems that the clinging snows only accentuate in winter. The framework of limb and twig is very different from that of the other trees, and the twisty lines seem to mean warmth and cheer, even against a frosty sky. And these old veterans are house trees, too--they do not suggest the forest or the broad expanse of nature, but, instead, the proximity of man and the home, the comfortable summer afternoon under their copious leafage, the great piles of ruddy-cheeked fruit in autumn.

I need hardly say anything of the apple-blossoms, for those who read these words are almost certain to have long appreciated their delicately fragrant blush and white loveliness. The apricot and the cherry are the first of the fruit trees to sing the spring song, and they cover themselves with white, in advance of any sign of green leaves on their twigs. The apple has an advantage; coming more deliberately, the little pink buds are set amidst the soft greens of the opening foliage, and the leaves and flowers expand together in their symphony of color and fragrance. The grass has grown lush by this time, the dandelions are punctuating it with gold, and everything is in the full riot of exuberant springtime.

But there are apples and apples and apples. Even the plain orchard gives us a difference in flowers, as well as in tree aspect. Notice the trees this coming May; mark the flat, white flowers on one tree, the cup-shaped, pink-veined blooms on another. Follow both through the fruiting, and see whether the sweeter flower brings the more sugary fruit. This fact ascertained, perhaps it may be followed up by observation of the distinctive color of the twigs and young branches--for there are wide differences in this respect, and the canny tree-grower knows his pets afar.

Perhaps there is a "crab" in the old orchard, ready to give the greatest burst of bloom--for the crab-apple flower is usually finer and more fragrant than any other of the cultivated forms. It is an especial refuge of the birds and the bees, you will find, and it invites them with its rare fragrance and deeper blush, so that they may work all the more earnestly at the pollination without which all this richness of bloom would be ineffective in nature's reproductive scheme.

This same crab-apple is soon to be, as its brilliant fruit matures, a notable object of beauty, for few ornamental trees can vie with its display of shining color. There was a great old crab right in the flower garden of my boyhood home, amid quaint box-trees, snowballs and lilacs. Lilies-of-the-valley flourished in its shadow, the delicate bleeding-heart mingled with old-fashioned irises and peonies at its feet. From early spring until mid-August the crab-apple held court of beauty there--and an always hungry boy often found something in addition to beauty in the red and yellow fruits that were acid but aromatic.

With a little attention, if one would plant crab-apples for their loveliness of fruit hue and form, a fine contrast of color may be had; for some varieties are perfect in clear yellow, against others in deepest scarlet, bloom-covered with blue haze, and yet others which carry all the colors from cream to crimson--the latter as the warm sun paints deeper.

Why do we not plant more fruit trees for beauty? Not one of our familiar fruits will fail us in this respect, if so considered. The apricot will often have its white flowers open to match the purity of the last snow, the cherry will follow with a burst of bloom, the apples and crab-apples will continue the show, aided by plum and pear and peach, and the quince--ah, there's a flower in a green enamel setting!--will close the blooming-time. But the cherry fruits now redden in shining roundness, the earlier apples throw rich gleams of color to the eye, and there is chromatic beauty until frost bids the last russets leave their stems, leaving bare the framework of the trees, to teach us in lines of symmetry and efficiency how strength and elegance are combined in nature's handiwork. Do you fear that some of the fruit may be taken? What of it? Plant for beauty, and the fruit is all extra--give it away freely, and pass on to others some of God's good gifts, to your own true happiness!

There is another crab-apple that is distinctive in its elegance, color and fragrance. It is the true "wild crab" of Eastern North America, and one who makes its acquaintance in blooming time will never forget it. The tree is not large, and it is likely to be set with crooked, thorny branches; but the flowers!

Deep pink or rosy red chalices, rather longer than the commonplace apple-blossom, and hanging on long and slender stems in a certain picturesquely stiff disposition, they are a joy for the senses of sight and fragrance. This notable native may be found on rich slopes and in dry glades--it is not fond of swamps. It is grown by some enlightened nurserymen, too, and can well be planted in the home grounds to their true adornment. The blossoms give way to form handsome yellow fruits, about an inch in diameter, which are themselves much more ornamental than edible, for even the small boy will not investigate a second time the bitter flesh. I have heard that a cider of peculiar "hardness" and potency, guaranteed to unsettle the firmest head, is made from these acid fruits--but I have not found it necessary to extend my tree studies in that direction.

The states west of Kansas do not know this lovely wild crab, to which the botanists give a really euphonious designation as Pyrus coronaria. There is a prairie-states crab-apple, which I have never seen, but which, I am told, has nothing like the beauty of our exquisite Eastern native. This Western species lacks the long stem and the bright color of the flowers of our favorite, and its fruits, while quite as viciously sour, are a dull and greasy green. The great West has many other things, but we have the wild crab-apple.

Rather between, as to beauty, is the native crab-apple of the Southland, which is known as the Soulard crab. It is not as attractive as our own Eastern gem, a pure native possession, and one which our foreign friends envy us.

Curiously enough, our own fruiting apple is not a native of America. It was at a meeting of a New England pomological association that I heard, several years ago, an old man of marvelous memory and power of observation tell of his recollections of seventy years, notable among which was his account of seeing the first good apples, as a boy, during a visit in the state of New York. Think of it! the most widely grown and beautiful of all our fruits hardly older than the railroad in America! We owe the apples we eat to Europe, for the start, the species being probably of Himalayan origin. America has greatly developed the apple, however, as one who has looked over the fruit tables at any great exposition will promptly testify, and nearly all our really good varieties are of American origin. Moreover, we are the greatest apple-growers in the world, and the yearly production probably exceeds a hundred millions of barrels.

The curious story of "Johnny Appleseed" is given us by historians, who tell us of this semi-religious enthusiast who roamed barefoot over the wilds of Ohio and Indiana a century ago, sowing apple-seeds in the scattered clearings, and living to see the trees bearing fruit, selections from which probably are interwoven among the varieties of today. New varieties of apples, by the way, come from seeds sown, and trees grown from them, with a bare chance that one in ten thousand may be worth keeping. When a variety seems thus worthy, "buds" or "scions" from the original tree are "budded" or "grafted" by the nurseryman into young seedling trees, which are thus changed into the selected sort. To sow the seeds of your favorite Baldwin does not imply that you will get Baldwin trees, by any means; you will more likely have a partial reversion to the acid and bitter original species.

It is not only for the fruit that we are indebted to the Old World, but also for some distinctively beautiful and most ornamental varieties of the apple, not by any means as well known among us as they ought to be. The nurserymen sell as an ornamental small tree a form known as "Parkman's double-flowering crab," which produces blooms of much beauty, like delicate little roses. Few of them, however, know of the glorious show that the spring brings where there is a proper planting of the Chinese and Japanese crab-apples, with some other hybrids and varieties. To readers in New England a pilgrimage to Boston is always in order. In the Public Gardens are superb specimens of these crab-apples from the Orient, as well as those native to this continent, and for several weeks in May they may be enjoyed. They are enjoyed by the Bostonians, who are in this, as in many things, better served by their authorities than is any other American city. What other city, for instance, gives its people such a magnificent spring show of hyacinths, tulips, daffodils and the like?

It is at the wonderful Arnold Arboretum, that Mecca of tree-lovers just outside of Boston and really within its superbly managed park system, that the greatest show of the "pyrus family," as the apples and pears are botanically called, may be found. Here have been gathered the lovely blooming trees of all the hardy world, to the delight of the eye and the nose, and the education of the mind. To me the most impressive of all was a wonderful Siberian crab (one must look for Pyrus baccata on the label, as the Arboretum folks are not in love with "common" names) close by the little greenhouses. Its round head was purely white, with no hint of pink, and the mass of bloom that covered it was only punctuated by the green of the expanding leaves. The especial elegance of this crab was in its whiteness, and that elegance was not diminished by the later masses of little yellow and red, almost translucent, fruits.

A somewhat smaller tree is commonly called the Chinese flowering apple, and its early flowers remind one strongly of the beauty of our own wild crab, as they are deeper in color than most of the crabs, being almost coral-red in bud. This "spectabilis," as it is familiarly called, is a gem, as it opens the season of the apple blooms with its burst of pink richness.

The beauty-loving Japanese have a festival at the time of the cherry-blooming--and it is altogether a festival of beauty, not connected with the food that follows the flowers. They actually dare to cut the blossoms, too, for adornment, and all the populace take time to drink in the message of the spring. Will we workaday Americans ever dare to "waste" so much time, and go afield to absorb God's provision of soul and sense refreshment in the spring, forgetting for the time our shops and desks, our stores and marts?

Professor Sargent, that deep student of trees who has built himself a monument, which is also a beneficence to all mankind, in the great volumes of his "Silva of North America," lives not far from Boston, and he loves especially that jewel of the apple family which, for want of a common name, I must designate scientifically as Pyrus floribunda. On his own magnificent estate, as well as at the Arboretum, this superb shrub or small tree riots in rosy beauty in early spring. While the leaves do come with these flowers, they are actually crowded back out of apparent sight by the straight wands of rose-red blooms, held by the twisty little tree at every angle and in indescribable beauty. If the visitor saw nothing but this Floribunda apple--"abundant flowering" sure enough--on his pilgrimage, he might well be satisfied, especially if he then and there resolved to see it again, either as he planted it at home or journeyed hither another spring for the enlargement of his soul.

There are other of these delightful crabs or apples to be enjoyed--Ringo, Kaido, Toringo--nearly all of Japanese origin, all of distinct beauty, and all continuing that beauty in handsome but inedible fruits that hang most of the summer. My tree-loving friends can well study these, and, I hope, plant them, instead of repeating continually the monotonously familiar shrubs and trees of ordinary commerce.

But I have not spoken enough of one notable feature of the every-day apple tree that we may see without a journey to the East. The fully set fruiting branch of an apple tree in health and vigor, properly nurtured and protected against fungous disease by modern "spraying," is a thing of beauty in its form and color. See those deep red Baldwins shine overhead in the frosty air of early fall; note the elegance of form and striping on the leathery-skinned Ben Davis; appreciate true apples of gold set in green enamel on a tree of the sunny Bellefleur! These in the fall; but it is hardly full summer before the closely set branches of Early Harvest are as beautiful as any orange-tree, or the more upright Red Astrachan is ablaze with fruit of red and yellow. Truly, an apple orchard might be arranged to give a series of pictures of changing beauty of color and growth from early spring until fall frost, and then to follow with a daily panorama of form and line against snow and sky until the blossoms peeped forth again. Let us learn, if we do not already love the apple tree, to love it for its beauty all the year!

Willows and Poplars

"By the rivers of Babylon, there we sat down, yea, we wept, when we remembered Zion. Upon the willows in the midst thereof we hanged our harps." Thus sang the Psalmist of the sorrows of the exiles in Babylon, and his song has fastened the name of the great and wicked city upon one of the most familiar willows, while also making it "weep"; for the common weeping willow is botanically named Salix Babylonica.

It may be that the forlorn Jews did hang their harps upon the tree we know as the weeping willow, that species being credited to Asia as a place of origin; but it is open to doubt, for the very obvious reason that the weeping willow is distinctly unadapted to use as a harp-rack, and one is at a loss to know just how the instruments in question would have been hung thereon. It is probable that the willows along the rivers of Babylon were of other species, and that the connection of the city of the captivity and the tears of the exiles with the long, drooping branches of the noble tree which has thus been sorrowfully named was a purely sentimental one. Indeed, the weeping willow is also called Napoleon's willow, because the great Corsican found much pleasure in a superb willow of the same species which stood on the lonely prison isle of St. Helena, and from twigs of which many trees in the United States have been grown.

The willow family presents great contrasts, both physical and sentimental. It is a symbol both of grief and of grace. The former characterization is undoubtedly because of the allusion of the one hundred and thirty-seventh Psalm, as quoted above, thoughtlessly extended through the centuries; and the latter, as when a beautiful and slender woman is said to be of "willowy" form, obviously because of the real grace of the long, swinging wands of the same tree. I might hint that a better reason for making the willow symbolize grief is because charcoal made from its twigs and branches is an important and almost essential ingredient of gunpowder, through which a sufficiency of grief has undoubtedly entered the world!

Willow twigs seem the very essence of fragility, as they break from the parent tree at a touch; and yet one of the willows furnishes the tough, pliable and enduring withes from which are woven the baskets of the world. The willows, usually thin in branch, sparse of somewhat pale foliage, of so-called mournful mien, are yet bursting with vigor and life; indeed, the spread and the value of the family is by reason of this tenacity and virility, which makes a broken twig, floating on the surface of a turbid stream, take root and grow on a sandy bank where nothing else can maintain itself, wresting existence and drawing strength and beauty from the very element whose ravages of flood and current it bravely withstands.

Apparently ephemeral in wood, growing quickly and perishing as quickly, the willows nevertheless supply us with an important preservative element, extracted from their bitter juices. Salicylic acid, made from willow bark, prevents change and arrests decay, and it is an important medical agent as well.

Flexible and seemingly delicate as the little tree is when but just established, there is small promise of the rugged and sturdy trunk that in a few years may stand where the chance twig lodged. And the color of the willows--ah! there's a point for full enthusiasm, for this family of grief furnishes a cheerful note for every month in the year, and runs the whole scale of greens, grays, yellows and browns, and even adds to the winter landscape touches of blazing orange and bright red across the snow. Before ever one has thought seriously of the coming of spring, the long branchlets of the weeping willow have quickened into a hint of lovely yellowish green, and those same branchlets will be holding their green leaves against a wintry blast when most other trees have given up their foliage under the frost's urgency. Often have the orange-yellow twigs of the golden osier illumined a somber countryside for me as I looked from the car window; and close by may be seen other willow bushes of brown, green, gray, and even purple, to add to the color compensation of the season. Then may come into the view, as one flies past, a great old weeping willow rattling its bare twigs in the wind; and, if a stream is passed, there are sure to be seen on its banks the sturdy trunks of the white and the black willows at least. Think of an average landscape with the willows eliminated, and there will appear a great vacancy not readily filled by another tree.

The weeping willow has always made a strong appeal to me, but never one of simple grief or sorrow. Its expression is rather of great dignity, and I remember watching in somewhat of awe one which grew near my childhood's home, as its branches writhed and twisted in a violent rain-storm, seeming then fairly to agonize, so tossed and buffeted were they by the wind. But soon the storm ceased, the sun shone on the rounded head of the willow, turning the raindrops to quickly vanishing diamonds, and the great tree breathed only a gentle and benignant peace. When, in later years, I came to know the moss-hung live-oak of the Southland, the weeping willow assumed to me a new dignity and value in the northern landscape, and I have strongly resented the attitude of a noted writer on "Art Out of Doors" who says of it: "I never once have seen it where it did not hurt the effect of its surroundings, or at least, if it stood apart from other trees, where some tree of another species would not have looked far better." One of the great merits of the tree, its difference of habit, its variation from the ordinary, is thus urged against it.

I have spoken of the basket willow, which is scientifically Salix viminalis, and an introduction from Europe, as indeed are many of the family. In my father's nursery grew a great patch of basket willows, annually cut to the ground to make a profusion of "sprouts," from which were cut the "tying willows" used to bind firmly together for shipment bundles of young trees. It was an achievement to be able to take a six-foot withe, and, deftly twisting the tip of it under the heel to a mass of flexible fiber, tie this twisted portion into a substantial loop; and to have this novel wooden rope then endure the utmost pull of a vigorous man, as he braced his feet against the bundle of trees in binding the withe upon it, gave an impression of anything but weakness on the part of the willow.

Who has not admired the soft gray silky buds of the "pussy" willow, swelling with the spring's impulse, and ripening quickly into a "catkin" loaded with golden pollen? Nowadays the shoots of this willow are "forced" into bud by the florists, and sold in the cities in great quantities; but really to see it one must find the low tree or bush by a stream in the woods, or along the roadside, with a chance to note its fullness of blossom. It is finest just when the hepaticas are at their bluest on the warm hillsides; and, one sunny afternoon of a spring journey along the north branch of the Susquehanna river, I did not know which of the two conspicuous ornaments of the deeply wooded bank made me most anxious to jump from the too swiftly moving train.

This pussy-willow has pleasing leaves, and is a truly ornamental shrub or small tree which will flourish quite well in a dry back yard, as I have reason to know. One bright day in February I found a pussy-willow tree, with its deep purple buds showing not a hint of the life within. The few twigs brought home quickly expanded when placed in water, and gave us their forecast of the spring. One twig was, out of curiosity, left in the water after the catkins had faded, merely to see what would happen. It bravely sent forth leaves, while at the base little white rootlets appeared. Its vigor appealing to us, it was planted in an arid spot in our back yard, and it is now, after a year and a half, a handsome, slender young tree that will give us a whole family of silken pussy-buds to stroke and admire another spring.

This same little tree is called also the glaucous willow, and it is botanically Salix discolor. It is more distinct than some others of the family, for the willow is a great mixer. The tree expert who will unerringly distinguish between the red oak and the scarlet oak by the precise angle of the spinose margins of the leaves (how I admire an accuracy I do not possess!) will balk at which is crack willow, or white willow, or yellow or blue willow. The abundant vigor and vitality and freedom of the family, and the fact that it is of what is known as the dioecious habit--that is, the flowers are not complete, fertile and infertile flowers being borne on separate trees--make it most ready to hybridize. The pollen of the black willow may fertilize the flower of the white willow, with a result that certainly tends to grayness on the worrying head of the botanist who, in after years, is trying to locate the result of the cross!

There is much variety in the willow flowers--and I wonder how many observers really notice any other willow "blossoms" than those of the showy pussy? A superb spring day afield took me along a fascinatingly crooked stream, the Conodoguinet, whose banks furnish a congenial and as yet protected (because concealed from the flower-hunting vandal) home for wild flowers innumerable and most beautiful, as well as trees that have ripened into maturity. An earlier visit at the time the bluebells were ringing out their silent message on the hillside, in exquisite beauty, with the lavender phlox fairly carpeting the woods, gave a glimpse of some promising willows on the other side of the stream. Twilight and letters to sign--how hateful the desk and its work seem in these days of springing life outside!--made a closer inspection impossible then, but a golden Saturday afternoon found three of us, of like ideals, hastening to this tree and plant paradise. A mass of soft yellow drew us from the highway across a field carpeted thickly with bluet or "quaker lady," to the edge of the stream, where a continuous hum showed that the bees were also attracted. It was one splendid willow in full bloom, and I could not and as yet cannot safely say whether it is the crack willow or the white willow; but I can affirm of a certainty that it was a delight to the eye, the mind and the nostrils. The extreme fragility of the smaller twigs, which broke away from the larger limbs at the lightest shake or jar, gave evidence of one of Nature's ways of distributing plant life; for it seems that these twigs, as I have previously said, part company with the parent tree most readily, float away on the stream, and easily establish themselves on banks and bars, where their tough, interlacing roots soon form an almost impregnable barrier to the onslaught of the flood. Only a stone's throw away there stood a great old black willow, with a sturdy trunk of ebon hue, crowned with a mass of soft green leafage, lighter where the breeze lifted up the under side to the sunlight. Many times, doubtless, the winds had shorn and the sleet had rudely trimmed this old veteran, but there remained full life and vigor, even more attractive than that of youth.

Most of the willows are shrubs rather than trees, and there are endless variations, as I have before remarked. Further, the species belonging at first in the Eastern Hemisphere have spread well over our own side of the globe, so that it seems odd to regard the white willow and the weeping willow as foreigners. At Niagara Falls, in the beautiful park on the American side, on the islands amid the toss of the waters, there are many willows, and those planted by man are no less beautiful than those resulting from Nature's gardening. In spring I have had pleasure in some splendid clumps of a form with lovely golden leaves and a small, furry catkin, found along the edge of the American rapids. I wonder, by the way, how many visitors to Niagara take note of the superb collection of plants and trees there to be seen, and which it is a grateful relief to consider when the mind is wearied with the majesty and the vastness of Nature's forces shown in the cataract? The birds are visitors to Goat Island and the other islets that divide the Niagara River, and they have brought there the plants of America in wonderful variety.

There is one willow that has been used by the nurserymen to produce a so-called weeping form, which, like most of these monstrosities, is not commendable. The goat willow is a vigorous tree introduced from Europe, having large and rather broad and coarse leaves, dark green above and whitish underneath. It is taken as a "stock," upon which, at a convenient height, the skilled juggler with trees grafts a drooping or pendulous form known as the Kilmarnock willow, thus changing the habit of the tree so that it then "weeps" to the ground. Fortunately, the original tree sometimes triumphs, the graft dies, and a lusty goat willow rears a rather shapely head to the sky.

This Kilmarnock willow is a favorite of the peripatetic tree agent, and I have enjoyed hugely one notable evidence of his persuasive eloquence to be seen in a Lebanon Valley town, inhabited by the quaint folk known as Pennsylvania Germans. All along the line of the railroad traversing this valley may be seen these distorted willows decorating the prim front yards, and they are not so offensive when used with other shrubs and trees. In this one instance, however, the tree agent evidently found a customer who was persuaded that if one Kilmarnock willow was a good thing to have, a dozen of them was twelve times better; wherefore his dooryard is grotesquely adorned with that many flourishing weepers, giving an aspect that is anything but decorous or solemn. Some time the vigilance of the citizen will be relaxed, it may be hoped; he will neglect to cut away the recurring shoots of the parent trees, and they will escape and destroy the weeping form which provides so much sarcastic hilarity for the passers-by.

The willow, with its blood relation, the poplar, is often "pollarded," or trimmed for wood, and its abundant vigor enables it to recover from this process of violent abbreviation more satisfactorily than do most trees. The result is usually a disproportionately large stem or bole, for the lopping off of great branches always tends to a thickening of the main stem. The abundant leafage of both willow and poplar soon covers the scars, and there is less cause to mourn than in the case of maples or other "hard-wooded" trees.

If my readers will only add a willow section to their mental observation outfit, there will be much more to see and appreciate. Look for and enjoy in the winter the variation in twig color and bark hue; notice how smoothly lies the covering on one stem, all rugged and marked on another. In the earliest spring examine the swelling buds, of widely differing color and character, from which shortly will spring forth the catkins or aments of bloom, followed by the leaves of varied colors in the varied species, and with shapes as varied. Vivid green, soft gray, greenish yellow; dull surface and shining surface above, pale green to almost pure white beneath; from the long and stringy leaf of the weeping willow to the comparatively broad and thick leaf of the pussy-willow--there is variety and interest in the foliage well worth the attention of the tree-lover. When winter comes, there will be another set of contrasts to see in the way the various species lose their leaves and get ready for the rest time during which the buds mature and ripen, and the winter colors again shine forth.

These observations may be made anywhere in America, practically, for the willow is almost indifferent to locality, growing everywhere that its far-reaching roots can find the moisture which it loves, and which it rapidly transpires to the thirsty air. As Miss Keeler well remarks, "The genus Salix is admirably fitted to go forth and inhabit the earth, for it is tolerant of all soils and asks only water. It creeps nearer to the North Pole than any other woody plant except its companion the birch. It trails upon the ground or rises one hundred feet in the air. In North America it follows the water-courses to the limit of the temperate zone, enters the tropics, crosses the equator, and appears in the mountains of Peru and Chili.... The books record one hundred and sixty species in the world, and these sport and hybridize to their own content and to the despair of botanists. Then, too, it comes of an ancient line;

for impressions of leaves in the cretaceous rocks show that it is one of the oldest of plants."

Common it is, and therefore overlooked; but the reader may well resolve to watch the willow in spring and summer, with its bloom and fruit; to follow its refreshing color through winter's chill; to observe its cheer and dignity; and to see the wind toss its slender wands and turn its graceful leaves.

The poplars and the willows are properly considered together, for together they form the botanical world family of the Salicace? Many characteristics of bloom and growth, of sap and bark, unite the two, and surely both, though alike common to the world, are common and familiar trees to the dwellers in North America.

One of my earliest tree remembrances has to do with a spreading light-leaved growth passed under every day on the way to school--and, like most school-boys, I was not unwilling to stop for anything of interest that might put off arrival at the seat of learning. This great tree had large and peculiar winter buds, that always seemed to have advance information as to the coming of spring, for they would swell out and become exceedingly shiny at the first touch of warm sun. Soon the sun-caressing would be responded to by the bursting of the buds, or the falling away of their ingenious outer protecting scales, which dropped to the ground, where, sticky and shining, and extraordinarily aromatic in odor, they were just what a curious school-boy enjoyed investigating. "Balm of Gilead" was the name that inquiry brought for this tree, and the resinous and sweet-smelling buds which preceded the rather inconspicuous catkins or aments of bloom seemed to justify the Biblical designation.

Nearly a world tree is this poplar, which in some one of its variable forms is called also tacamahac, and balsam poplar as well. Its cheerful upright habit, really fine leaves and generally pleasing air commend it, but there is one trouble--it is almost too vigorous and anxious to spread, which it does by means of shoots or "suckers," upspringing from its wide area of root-growth, thus starting a little forest of its own that gives other trees but small chance. But on a street, where the repression of pavements and sidewalks interferes with this exuberance, the balsam poplar is well worth planting.

The poplars as a family are pushing and energetic growers, and serve a great purpose in the reforestation of American acres that have been carelessly denuded of their tree cover. Here the trembling aspen particularly, as the commonest form of all is named, comes in to quickly cover and shade the ground, and give aid to the hard woods and the conifers that form the value of the forest growth.

This same American aspen, a consideration of the lightly hung leaves of which has been useful to many poets, is a well-known tree of graceful habit, particularly abundant in the forests north of Pennsylvania and New Jersey, and occupying clearings plentifully and quickly. Its flowers are in catkins, as with the rest of the family, and, like other poplars, they are in two kinds, male and female, or staminate and pistillate, which accounts for some troubles the inexperienced investigator has in locating them.

There is another aspen, the large-toothed form, that is a distinct botanical species; but I have never been able to separate it, wherefore I do not try to tell of it here, lest I fall under condemnation as a blind leader, not of the blind, but of those who would see!

In many cities, especially in cities that have experienced real-estate booms, and have had "extensions" laid out "complete with all improvements," there is to be seen a poplar that has the merit of quick and pleasing growth and considerable elegance as well. Alas, it is like the children of the tropics in quick beauty and quick decadence! The Carolina poplar, it is called, being a variety of the wide-spread cottonwood. Grow? All that is needed is to cut a lusty branch of it, point it, and drive it into the earth--it will do the rest!

This means cheap trees and quick growth, and that is why whole new streets in West Philadelphia, for instance, are given up to the Carolina poplar. Its clear, green, shining leaves, of good size, coming early in spring; its easily guided habit, either upright or spreading; its very rapid growth, all commend it. But its coarseness and lack of real strength, and its continual invitation to the tree-butcher and the electric lineman, indicate the undesirability of giving it more than a temporary position, to shade while better trees are growing.

But I must not get into the economics of street-tree planting. I started to tell of the blossoms of this same Carolina poplar, which are decidedly interesting.

Just when the sun has thoroughly warmed up the air of spring there is a sudden, rapid thickening of buds over one's head on this poplar. One year the tree under my observation swelled and swelled its buds, which were shining more and more in the sun, until I was sure the next day would bring a burst of leaves. But the weather was dry, and it was not until that wonderful solvent and accelerator of growing things, a warm spring rain, fell softly upon the tree, that the pent-up life force was given vent. Then came, not leaves, but these long catkins, springing out with great rapidity, until in a few hours the tree glowed with their redness. A second edition of the shower, falling sharply, brought many of the catkins to the ground, where they lay about like large caterpillars.

The whole process of this blooming was interesting, curious, but hardly beautiful, and it seemed to fit in with the restless character of the poplar family--a family of trees with more vigor than dignity, more sprightliness than grace. As Professor Bailey says of the cottonwood, "It is cheerful and restive. One is not moved to lie under it as he is under a maple or an oak." Yet there are not wanting some poplars of impressive character.

One occurs to me, growing on a wide street of my home town, opposite a church with a graceful spire. This white or silver-leaved poplar has for many years been a regular prey of the gang of tree-trimmers, utterly without knowledge of or regard for trees, that infests this town. They hack it shamefully, and I look at it and say, "Well, the old poplar is ruined now, surely!" But a season passes, and I look again, to see that the tremendous vigor of the tree has triumphed over the butchers; its sores have been concealed, new limbs have pushed out, and it has again, in its unusual height, assumed a dignity not a whit inferior to that of the church spire opposite.

This white poplar is at its best on the bank of a stream, where its small forest of "suckers" most efficiently protects the slope against the destructive action of floods. One such tree with its family and friends I saw in full bloom along the Susquehanna, and it gave an impression of solidity and size, as well as of lusty vigor, and I have always liked it since. The cheerful bark is not the least of its attractions--but it is a tree for its own place, and not for every place, by reason of the tremendous colonizing power of its root-sprouts.

I wonder, by the way, if many realize the persistence and vigor of the roots of a tree of the "suckering" habit? Some years ago an ailanthus, a tree of vigor and beauty of foliage but nastiness of flower odor, was cut away from its home when excavation was being made for a building, which gave me opportunity to follow a few of its roots. One of them traveled in search of food, and toward the opportunity of sending up a shoot, over a hundred feet!

The impending scarcity of spruce logs to feed the hungry maws of the machines that make paper for our daily journals has turned attention to several forms of the rapid-growing poplar for this use. The aspen is acceptable, and also the Carolina poplar, and these trees are being planted in large quantities for the eventual making of wood-pulp. Even today, many newspapers are printed on poplar, and exposure to the rays of the truth-searching sun for a few hours will disclose the yellowness of the paper, if not of the tree from which it has been ground.

Few whose eyes are turned upward toward the trees have failed to note that exclamation-point of growth, the Lombardy poplar. Originating in that portion of Europe indicated by its common name, and, indeed, a botanical form of the European black poplar, it is nevertheless widely distributed in America. When it has been properly placed, it introduces truly a note of distinction into the landscape. Towering high in the air, and carrying the eye along its narrowly oval contour to a skyward point, it is lofty and pleasing in a park. It agreeably breaks the sky-line in many places, and is emphatic in dignified groups. To plant it in rows is wrong; and I say this as an innocent offender myself. In boyhood I lived along the banks of the broad but shallow Susquehanna, and enjoyed the boating possible upon that stream when it was not reduced, as graphically described by a disgusted riverman, to merely a heavy dew. Many times I lost my way returning to the steep bluff near my home after the sun had gone to rest, and a hard pull against the swift current would ensue as I skirted the bank, straining eyes for landmarks in the dusk. It occurred to me to plant six Lombardy poplars on the top of the bluff, which might serve as easily recognized landmarks. Four of them grew, and are now large trees, somewhat offensive to a quickened sense of appropriateness. Long since the old home has been swallowed up by the city's advance, and I suppose none who now see those four spires of green on the river-bank even guess at the reason for their existence.

The poplar family, as a whole, is exuberant with vigor, and interesting more on that account than by reason of its general dignity or strength or elegance. It is well worth a little attention and study, and the consideration particularly of its bloom periods, to which I commend the tree-sense of my readers as they take the tree walks that ought to punctuate these chapters.

The Elm and the Tulip

America has much that is unique in plant and tree growth, as one learns who sees first the collections of American plants shown with pride by acute gardeners and estate owners in England and on the European Continent. Many a citizen of our country must needs confess with some shame that his first estimation of the singular beauty of the American laurel has been born in England, where the imported plants are carefully nurtured; and the European to whom the rhododendrons of his own country and of the Himalayas are familiar is ready to exclaim in rapture at the superb effect and tropical richness of our American species, far more lusty and more truly beautiful here than the introductions which must be heavily paid for and constantly coddled.

For no trees, however, may Americans feel more pride than for our American elms and our no less American tulip, the latter miscalled tulip "poplar." Both are trees practically unique to the country, both are widespread over Eastern North America, both are thoroughly trees of the people, both attain majestic proportions, both are long-lived and able to endure much hardship without a full giving up of either beauty or dignity.

The American elm--how shall I properly speak of its exceeding grace and beauty! In any landscape it introduces an element of distinction and elegance not given by any other tree. Looking across a field at a cluster of trees, there may be a doubt as to the identity of an oak, a chestnut, a maple, an ash, but no mistake can be made in regard to an elm--it stands alone in the simple elegance of its vase-like form, while its feathery branchlets, waving in the lightest breeze, add to the refined and classic effect. I use the word "classic" advisedly, because, although apparently out of place in describing a tree, it nevertheless seems needed for the form of the American elm.

The elm is never rugged as is the oak, but it gives no impression of effeminacy or weakness. Its uprightness is forceful and strong, and its clean and shapely bole impresses the beholder as a joining of gently outcurving columns, ample in strength and of an elegance belonging to itself alone. If I may dare to compare man-made architectural forms with the trees that graced the garden of Eden, I would liken the American elm (it is also the water elm and the white elm, and botanically Ulmus Americana) to the Grecian types, combining stability with elegance, rather than to the more rugged works of the Goths. Yet the free swing of the elm's wide-spreading branches inevitably suggests the pointed Gothic arch in simplicity and obvious strength.

It is difficult to say when the American elm is most worthy of admiration. In summer those same arching branches are clothed and tipped with foliage of such elegance and delicacy as the form of the tree would seem to predicate. The leaf itself is ornate, its straight ribs making up a serrated and pointed oval form of the most interesting character. These leaves hang by slender stems, inviting the gentlest zephyr to start them to singing of comfort in days of summer heat. The elm is fully clothed down to the drooping tips of the branchlets with foliage, which, though deepest green above, reflects, under its dense shade, a soft light from the paler green of the lower side. It is no wonder that New England claims fame for her elms, which, loved and cared for, arch over the long village streets that give character to the homes of the descendants of the Puritan fathers. The fully grown elm presents to the sun a darkly absorbent hue, and to the passer-by who rests beneath its shade the most grateful and restful color in all the rainbow's palette.

Then, too, the evaporative power of these same leaves is simply enormous, and generally undreamed of. Who would think that a great, spreading elm, reaching into the air of August a hundred feet, and shading a circle of nearly as great diameter, was daily cooling the atmosphere with tons of water, silently drawn from the bosom of Mother Earth!

Like many other common trees, the American elm blooms almost unnoticed. When the silver maple bravely pushes out its hardy buds in earliest spring--or often in what might be called latest winter--the elm is ready, and the sudden swelling of the twigs, away above our heads in March or April, is not caused by the springing leaves, but is the flowering effort of this noble tree. The bloom sets curiously about the yet bare branches, and the little brownish yellow or reddish flowers are seemingly only a bunch of stamens. They do their work promptly, and the little flat fruits, or "samaras," are ripened and dropped before most of us realize that the spring is fully upon us. These seeds germinate readily, and I recall the great pleasure with which a noted horticultural professor showed me what he called his "elm lawn," one summer. It seemed that almost every one of the thousands of seeds that, just about the time his preparations for sowing a lawn were completed, had softly fallen from the great elm which guards and shades his dooryard, had found good ground, and the result was a miniature forest of tiny trees, giving an effect of solid green which was truly a tree lawn.

But, after all, I think it is in winter that the American elm is at its finest, for then stand forth most fully revealed the wonderful symmetry of its structure and the elegance of its lines. It has one advantage in its great size, which is well above the average, for it lifts its graceful head a hundred feet or more above the earth. The stem is usually clean and regular, and the branches spread out in closely symmetrical relation, so that, as seen against the cold sky of winter, leafless and bare, they seem all related parts of a most harmonious whole. Other great trees are notable for the general effect of strength or massiveness, individual branches departing much from the average line of the whole structure; but the American elm is regular in all its parts, as well as of general stateliness.

As I have noted, the people of the New England States value and cherish their great elms, and they are accustomed to think themselves the only possessors of this unique tree. We have, however, as good elms in Pennsylvania as there are in New England, and I hope the day is not far distant when we shall esteem them as highly. The old elm monarch which stands at the gingerbread brownstone entrance of the Capitol Park in Pennsylvania's seat of government has had a hard battle, defenseless as it is, against the indifference of those whom it has shaded for generations, and who carelessly permitted the telegraph and telephone linemen to use it or chop it at their will. But latterly there has been an awakening which means protection, I think, for this fine old landmark.

The two superb elms, known as "Paul and Virginia," that make notable the north shore of the Susquehanna at Wilkesbarre, are subjects of local pride; which seems, however, not strong enough to prevent the erection of a couple of nasty little shanties against their great trunks. There can be no doubt, however, that the sentiment of reverence for great trees, and of justice to them for their beneficent influence, is spreading westward and southward from New England. It gives me keen pleasure to learn of instances where paths, pavements or roadways have been changed, to avoid doing violence to good trees; and a recent account of the creation of a trust fund for the care of a great oak, as well as a unique instance in Georgia, where a deed has been recorded giving a fine elm a quasi-legal title to its own ground, show that the rights of trees are coming to be recognized.

I have said little of the habitat, as the botanist puts it, of the American elm. It graces all North America east of the Rockies, and the specimens one sees in Michigan or Canada are as happy, apparently, as if they grew in Connecticut or in Virginia. Our increasingly beautiful national Capital, the one city with an intelligent and controlled system of tree-planting, shows magnificent avenues of flourishing elms.

But I must not forget some other elms, beautiful and satisfactory in many places. It is no discredit to our own American elm to say that the English elm is a superb tree in America. It seems to be characteristically British in its sturdy habit, and forms a grand trunk.

The juicy inner bark of the red or "slippery" elm was always acceptable, in lieu of the chewing-gum which had not then become so common, to a certain ever-hungry boy who used to think as much of what a tree would furnish that was eatable as he now does of its beauty. Later, the other uses of the bark of this tree became known to the same boy, but it was many years before he came really to know the slippery elm. One day a tree branch overhead showed what seemed to be remarkable little green flowers, which on examination proved to be, instead, the very interesting fruit of this elm, each little seed securely held inside a very neat and small flat bag. Looking at it earlier the next spring, the conspicuous reddish brown color of the bud-scales was noted.

I have never seen the "wahoo," or winged elm of the South, and there are several other native elms, as well as a number of introductions from the Eastern Hemisphere, with which acquaintance is yet to be made. All of them together, I will maintain with the quixotic enthusiasm of lack of knowledge, are not worth as much as one-half hour spent in looking up under the leafy canopy of our own preeminent American elm--a tree surely among those given by the Creator for the healing of the nations.

The tulip-tree, so called obviously because of the shape of its flowers, has a most mellifluous and pleasing botanical name, Liriodendron Tulipifera--is not that euphonious? Just plain "liriodendron"--how much better that sounds as a designation for one of the noblest of American forest trees than the misleading "common" names! "Tulip-tree," for a resemblance of the form only of its extraordinary blooms; "yellow poplar," probably because it is not yellow, and is in no way related to the poplars; and "whitewood," the Western name, because its wood is whiter than that of some other native trees. "Liriodendron" translated means "lily-tree," says my learned friend who knows Greek, and that is a fitting designation for this tree, which proudly holds forth its flowers, as notable and beautiful as any lily, and far more dignified and refined than the gaudy tulip. I like to repeat this smooth-sounding, truly descriptive and dignified name for a tree worthy all admiration. Liriodendron! Away with the "common" names, when there is such a pleasing scientific cognomen available!

By the way, why should people who will twist their American tongues all awry in an attempt to pronounce French words in which the necessary snort is unexpressed visually and half the characters are "silent," mostly exclaim at the alleged difficulty of calling trees and plants by their world names, current among educated people everywhere, while preferring some misleading "common" name? Very few scientific plant names are as difficult to pronounce as is the word "chrysanthemum," and yet the latter comes as glibly from the tongue as do "geranium," "rhododendron," and the like. Let us, then, at least when we have as good a name as liriodendron for so good a tree, use it in preference to the most decidedly "common" names that belie and mislead.

I have said that this same tulip-tree--which I will call liriodendron hereafter, at a venture--is a notable American tree, peculiar to this country. So believed the botanists for many years, until an inquiring investigator found that China, too, had the same tree, in a limited way. We will still claim it as an American native, and tell the Chinamen they are fortunate to have such a superb tree in their little-known forests. They have undoubtedly taken advantage, in their art forms, of its peculiarly shaped leaves, if not of the flowers and the curious "candlesticks" that succeed them.

Let us consider this liriodendron first as a forest tree, as an inhabitant of the "great woods" that awed the first intelligent observers from Europe, many generations back. Few of our native trees reach such a majestic height, here on the eastern side of the continent, its habitat. Ordinarily it builds its harmonious structure to a height of seventy or a hundred feet; but occasional individuals double this altitude, and reach a trunk diameter of ten feet. While in the close forest it towers up with a smooth, clean bole, in open places it assumes its naturally somewhat conical form very promptly. Utterly dissimilar in form from the American elm, it seems to stand for dignity, solidity and vigor, and yet to yield nothing in the way of true elegance. The botanists tell us it prefers deep and moist soil, but I know that it lives and seems happy in many soils and in many places. Always and everywhere it shows a clean, distinct trunk, its brown bark uniformly furrowed, but in such a manner as to give a nearly smooth appearance at a little distance. The branches do not leave the stem so imperceptibly as do those which give the elm its very distinct form, but rather start at a right angle, leaving the distinct central column of solid strength unimpaired. The winter tracery of these branches, and the whole effect of the liriodendron without foliage, is extremely distinct and pleasing. I have in mind a noble group of great liriodendrons which I first saw against an early April sky of blue and white. The trees had grown close, and had interlaced their somewhat twisty branches, so that the general impression was that of one great tree supported on several stems. The pure beauty of these very tall and very stately trees, thus grouped and with every twig sharply outlined, I shall always remember.

The liriodendron is more fortunate than some other trees, for it has several points of attractiveness. Its stature and its structure are alike notable, its foliage entirely unique, and its flowers and seed-pods even more interesting. The leaf is very easily recognized when once known. It is large, but not in any way coarse, and is thrust forth as the tree grows, in a peculiarly pleasing way. Sheathed in the manner characteristic of the magnolia family, of which the liriodendron is a notable member, the leaves come to the light practically folded back on themselves, between the two protecting envelopes, which remain until the leaf has stretched out smoothly. Yellowish green at first, they rapidly take on the bright, strong green of maturity. The texture is singularly refined, and it is a pleasure to handle these smooth leaves, of a shape which stamps them at once on the memory, and of a coloring, both above and below, that is most attractive. They are maintained on long, slender stems, or "petioles," and these stems give a great range of flexibility, so that the leaves of the liriodendron are, as Henry Ward Beecher puts it, "intensely individual, each one moving to suit himself."

Of course all this moving, and this out-breaking of the leaves from their envelopes, take place far above one's head, on mature trees. It will be found well worth while, however, for the tree-lover to look in the woods for the rather numerous young trees of the tulip, and to observe the very interesting way in which the growth proceeds. The beautiful form and color of the leaves may also be thus conveniently noted, as also in the autumn the soft, clear yellow early assumed.

It is the height and spread of the liriodendron that keep its truly wonderful flowers out of the public eye. If they were produced on a small tree like the familiar dogwood, for instance, so that they might be nearer to the ground, they would receive more of the admiration so fully their due. In Washington, where, as I have said, trees are planted by design and not at random, there are whole avenues of liriodendrons, and it was my good fortune one May to drive between these lines of strong and shapely young trees just when they were in full bloom. The appearance of these beautiful cups, each one held upright, not drooping, was most striking and elegant. Some time, other municipalities will learn wisdom from the example set in Washington, and we may expect to see some variety in our street trees, now monotonously confined for the most part to the maples, poplars, and a few good trees that would be more valued if interspersed with other equally good trees of different character. The pin-oak, the elm, the sweet-gum, or liquidambar, the ginkgo, and a half-dozen or more beautiful and sturdy trees, do admirably for street planting, and ought to be better known and much more freely used.

I have seen many rare orchids brought thousands of miles and petted into a curious bloom--indeed, often more curious than beautiful. If the bloom of the liriodendron, in all its delicate and daring mingling of green and yellow, cream and orange, with its exquisite interior filaments, could be labeled as a ten-thousand-dollar orchid beauty from Borneo, its delicious perfume would hardly be needed to complete the raptures with which it would be received into fashionable flower society. But these lovely cups stand every spring above our heads by millions, their fragrance and form, their color and beauty, unnoticed by the throng. As they mature into the brown fruit-cones that hold the seeds, and these in turn fall to the ground, to fulfil their purpose of reproduction, there is no week in which the tree is not worthy of attention; and, when the last golden leaf has been plucked by the fingers of the winter's frost, there yet remain on the bare branches the curious and interesting candlestick-like outer envelopes of the fruit-cones, to remind us in form of the wonderful flower, unique in its color and attractiveness, that gave its sweetness to the air of May and June.

These two trees--the elm and the liriodendron--stand out strongly as individuals in the wealth of our American trees. Let all who read and agree in my estimate, even in part, also agree to try, when opportunity offers, to preserve these trees from vandalism or neglect, realizing that the great forest trees of our country are impossible of replacement, and that their strength, majesty and beauty are for the good of all.

Nut-Bearing Trees

What memories of chestnutting parties, of fingers stained with the dye of walnut hulls, and of joyous tramps afield in the very heart of the year, come to many of us when we think of the nuts of familiar knowledge! Hickory-nuts and butternuts, too, perhaps hazelnuts and even beechnuts--all these American boys and girls of the real country know. In the far South, and, indeed, reaching well up into the Middle West, the pecan holds sway, and a majestic sway at that, for its size makes it the fellow of the great trees of the forest, worthy to be compared with the chestnut, the walnut, and the hickory.

But it has usually been of nuts to eat that we have thought, and the chance for palatable food has, just as with some of the best of the so-called "fruit" trees--all trees bear fruit!--partially closed our eyes to the interest and beauty of some of these nut-bearers.

My own tree acquaintance has proceeded none too rapidly, and I have been--and am yet--as fond of the toothsome nuts as any one can be who is not a devotee of the new fad that attempts to make human squirrels of us all by a nearly exclusive nut diet. I think that my regard for a nut tree as something else than a source of things to eat began when I came, one hot summer day, under the shade of the great walnut at Paxtang. Huge was its trunk and wide the spread of its branches, while the richness of its foliage held at bay the strongest rays of the great luminary. How could I help admiring the venerable yet lusty old tree, conferring a present benefit, giving an instant and restful impression of strength, solidity, and elegance, while promising as well, as its rounded green clusters hung far above my head, a great crop of delicious nut-fruit when the summer's sun it was so fully absorbing should have done its perfect work!

Alas for the great black walnut of Paxtang! It went the way of many another tree monarch whose beauty and living usefulness were no defense against sordid vandalism. In the course of time a suburb was laid out, including along its principal street, and certainly as its principal natural ornament, this massive tree, around which the Indians who roamed the "great vale of Pennsylvania" had probably gathered in council. The sixty-foot "lot," the front of which the tree graced, fell to the ownership of a man who, erecting a house under its beneficent protection, soon complained of its shade. Then came a lumber prospector, who saw only furniture in the still flourishing old black walnut. His offer of forty dollars for the tree was eagerly accepted by the Philistine who had the title to the land, and although there were not wanting such remonstrances as almost came to a breaking of the peace, the grand walnut ended its hundreds of years of life to become mere lumber for its destroyers! The real estate man who sold the land greatly admired the tree himself, realizing also its great value to the suburb, and had never for one moment dreamed that the potential vandal who bought the tree-graced parcel of ground would not respect the inherent rights of all his neighbors. He told me of the loss with tears in his eyes and rage in his language; and I have never looked since at the fellow who did the deed without reprobation. More than that, he has proven a theory I hold--that no really good man would do such a thing after he had been shown the wrong of it--by showing himself as dishonest in business as he was disregardful of the rights of the tree and of his neighbors.

The black walnut is a grand tree from any point of view, even though it so fully absorbs all water and fertility as to check other growth under its great reach of branches. The lines it presents to the winter sky are as rugged as those of the oak, but there is a great difference. And this ruggedness is held far into the spring, for the black walnut makes no slightest apparent effort at growth until all the other trees are greening the countryside. Then with a rush come the luxuriant and tropical compound leaves, soon attaining their full dignity, and adding to it also a smooth polish on the upper surface. The walnut's flowers I have missed seeing, I am sorry to say, while registering a mental promise not to permit another season to pass without having that pleasure.

Late in the year the foliage has become scanty, and the nut-clusters hang fascinatingly clear, far above one's head, to tempt the climb and the club. The black walnut is a tree that needs our care; for furniture fashion long used its close-grained, heavy, handsome wood as cruelly as the milliners did the herons of Florida from which were torn the "aigrets," now happily "out of style." Though walnut furniture is no longer the most popular, the deadly work has been done, for the most part, and but few of these wide-spread old forest monarchs yet remain. Scientific forestry is now providing, in many plantings, and in many places, another "crop" of walnut timber, grown to order, and using waste land. It is to such really beneficent, though entirely commercial work, that we must look for the future of many of our best trees.

The butternut, or white walnut, has never seemed so interesting to me, nor its fruit so palatable, probably because I have seen less of it. The so-called "English" walnut, which is really the Persian walnut, is not hardy in the eastern part of the United States, and, while a tree of vast commercial importance in the far West, does not come much into the view of a lover of the purely American trees.

Of the American sweet chestnut as a delightful nut-fruit I need say nothing more than that it fully holds its place against "foreign intervention" from the East; even though these European and Japanese chestnuts with their California-bred progeny give us fruit that is much larger, and borne on trees of very graceful habit. No one with discrimination will for a moment hesitate, after eating a nut of both, to cheerfully choose the American native as best worth his commendation, though he may come to understand the food value, after cooking, of the chestnuts used so freely in parts of Europe.

As a forest tree, however, our American sweet chestnut has a place of its own. Naturally spreading in habit when growing where there is room to expand, it easily accommodates itself to the more cramped conditions of our great woodlands, and shoots upward to light and air, making rapidly a clean and sturdy stem. What a beautiful and stately tree it is! And when, late in the spring, or indeed right on the threshold of summer, its blooming time comes, it stands out distinctly, having then few rivals in the eye of the tree-lover. The locust and the tulip are just about done with their floral offering upon the altar of the year when the long creamy catkins of the sweet chestnut spring out from the fully perfected dark green leaf-clusters. Peculiarly graceful are these great bloom heads, high in the air, and standing nearly erect, instead of hanging down as do the catkins of the poplars and the birches. The odor of the chestnut flower is heavy, and is best appreciated far above in the great tree, where it may mingle with the warm air of June, already bearing a hundred sweet scents.

There stands bright in my remembrance one golden June day when I came through a gateway into a wonderful American garden of purely native plants maintained near Philadelphia, the rock-bound drive guarded by two clumps of tall chestnuts, one on either side, and both in full glory of bloom. There could not have been a more beautiful, natural, or dignified entrance; and it was just as beautiful in the early fall, when the deep green of the oblong-toothed leaves had changed to clear and glowing yellow, while the flowers had left their perfect work in the swelling and prickly green burs which hid nuts of a brown as rich as the flesh was sweet.

Did you, gentle reader, ever saunter through a chestnut grove in the later fall, when the yellow had been browned by the frosts which brought to the ground alike leaves and remaining burs? There is something especially pleasant in the warmth of color and the crackle of sound on the forest floor, as one really shuffles through chestnut leaves in the bracing November air, stooping now and then for a nut perchance remaining in the warm and velvety corner of an opened bur.

Here in Pennsylvania, and south of Mason and Dixon's line, there grows a delightful small tree, brother to the chestnut, bearing especially sweet little nuts which we know as chinquapins. They are darker brown, and the flesh is very white, and rich in flavor. I could wish that the chinquapin, as well as the chestnut, was included among the trees that enlightened Americans would plant along roadsides and lanes, with other fruit trees; the specific secondary purpose, after the primary enjoyment of form, foliage and flower, being to let the future passer-by eat freely of that fruit provided by the Creator for food and pleasure, and costing no more trouble or expense than the purely ornamental trees more frequently planted.

Both chestnut and chinquapin are beautiful ornamental trees; and some of the newer chestnut hybrids, of parentage between the American and the European species, are as graceful as the most highly petted lawn trees of the nurserymen. Indeed, the very same claim may be made for a score or more of the standard fruit trees, alike beautiful in limb tracery, in bloom, and in the seed-coverings that we are glad to eat; and some time we shall be ashamed not to plant the fruit trees in public places, for the pleasure and the refreshing of all who care.

One of the commonest nut trees, and certainly one of the most pleasing, is the hickory. There are hickories and hickories, and some are shellbarks, while others are bitternuts or pignuts. The form most familiar to the Eastern States is the shagbark hickory, and its characteristic upright trees, tall and finely shaped, never wide-spreading as is the chestnut under the encouragement of plenty of room and food, are admirable from any standpoint. There is a lusty old shagbark in Wetzel's Swamp that has given me many a pleasant quarter-hour, as I have stood at attention before its symmetrical stem, hung with slabs of brown bark that seem always just ready to separate from the trunk.

The aspect of this tree is reflected in its very useful timber, which is pliant but tough, requiring less "heft" for a given strength, and bending with a load easily, only to instantly snap back to its position when the stress slackens. Good hickory is said to be stronger than wrought iron, weight for weight; and I will answer for it that no structure of iron can ever have half the grace, as well as strength, freely displayed by this same old shagbark of the lowlands near my home.

Curious as I am to see the blooms of the trees I am getting acquainted with, there are many disappointments to be endured--as when the favorite tree under study is reached a day too late, and I must wait a year for another opportunity. It was, therefore, with much joy that I found that a trip carefully timed for another fine old hickory along the Conodoguinet--an Indian-named stream of angles, curves, many trees and much beauty--had brought me to the quickly passing bloom feast of this noble American tree. The leaves were about half-grown and half-colored, which means that they displayed an elegance of texture and hue most pleasing to see. And the flowers--there they were, hanging under the twigs in long clusters of what I might describe as ends of chenille, if it were not irreverent to compare these delicate greenish catkins with anything man-made!

This fine shagbark was kind to the cameraman, for some of its lower branches drooped and hung down close enough to the "bars" of the rail fence to permit the photographic eye to be turned on them. Then came the tantalizing wait for stillness! I have frequently found that a wind, absolutely unnoticeable before, became obtrusively strong just when the critical moment arrived, and I have fancied that the lightly hung leaflets I have waited upon fairly shook with merriment as they received the gentle zephyr, imperceptible to my heated brow, but vigorous enough to keep them moving. Often, too--indeed nearly always--I have found that after exhausting my all too scanty stock of patience, and making an "exposure" in despair, the errant blossoms and leaflets would settle down into perfect immobility, as if to say, "There! don't be cross--we'll behave," when it was too late.

But the shagbark at last was good to me, and I could leave with the comfortable feeling that I was carrying away a little bit of nature's special work, a memorandum of her rather private processes of fruit-making, without injuring any part of the inspected trees. It has been a sorrow to me that I have not seen that great hickory later in the year, when the clusters of tassels have become bunches of husk-covered nuts. To get really acquainted with any tree, it should be visited many times in a year. Starting with the winter view, one observes the bark, the trend and character of the limbs, the condition of the buds. The spring opening of growth brings rapid changes, of both interest and beauty, to be succeeded by the maturity of summer, when, with the ripened foliage overhead, everything is different. Again, when the fruit is on, and the touch of Jack Frost is baring the tree for the smoother passing of the winds of winter, there is another aspect. I have great respect for the tree-lover who knows unerringly his favorites at any time of the year, for have I not myself made many mistakes, especially when no leaves are at hand as pointers? The snow leaves nothing to be seen but the cunning framework of the tree--tell me, then, is it ash, or elm, or beech? Which is sugar-maple, and which red, or sycamore?

One summer walk in the deep forest, my friend the doctor, who knows many things besides the human frame, was puzzled at a sturdy tree bole, whose leaves far overhead mingled so closely with the neighboring greenery of beech and birch that in the dim light they gave no help. First driving the small blade of his pocket-knife deep into the rugged bark of the tree in question, he withdrew it, and then smelled and tasted, exclaiming, "Ah, I thought so; it is the wild cherry!" And, truly, the characteristic prussic-acid odor, the bitter taste, belonging to the peach and cherry families, were readily noted; and another Sherlock Holmes tree fact came to me!

Of other hickories I know little, for the false shagbark, the mockernut, the pignut, and the rest of the family have not been disclosed to me often enough to put me at ease with them. There are to be more tree friends, both human and arborescent, and more walks with the doctor and the camera, I hope!

We of the cold North, as we crack the toothsome pecan, hardly realize its kinship with the hickory. It is full brother to our shellbark, which is, according to botany, Hicoria ovata, while the Southern tree is Hicoria pecan. A superb tree it is, too, reaching up amid its vigorous associates of the forests of Georgia, Alabama and Texas to a height exceeding one hundred and fifty feet. Its upright and elegant form, of a grace that conceals its great height, its remarkable usefulness, and its rather rapid growth, commend it highly. The nut-clusters are striking, having not only an interesting outline, but much richness of color, in greens and russets.

It may seem odd to include the beech under the nut-bearing trees, to those of us who know only the nursery-grown forms of the European beech, "weeping" and twisted, with leaves of copper and blood, as seen in parks and pleasure-grounds. But the squirrels would agree; they know well the sweet little triangular nuts that ripen early in fall.

The pure American beech, uncontaminated and untwisted with the abnormal forms just mentioned, is a tree that keeps itself well in the eye of the woods rambler; and that eye is always pleasured by it, also. Late in winter, the light gray branches of a beech thicket on a dry hillside on the edge of my home city called attention to their clean elegance amid sordid and forbidding surroundings, and it was with anger which I dare call righteous that I saw a hideous bill-board erected along the hillside, to shut out the always beautiful beeches from sight as I frequently passed on a trolley car! I have carefully avoided buying anything of the merchants who have thus set up their announcements where they are an insult; and it might be noted that these and other offensive bill-boards are to others of like mind a sort of reverse advertising--they tell us what not to purchase.

Years ago I chanced to be present at a birth of beech leaves, up along Paxton Creek. It was late in the afternoon, and our reluctant feet were turning homeward, after the camera had seen the windings of the creek against the softening light, when the beeches over-arching the little stream showed us this spring marvel. The little but perfectly formed leaves had just opened, in pairs, with a wonderful covering of silvery green, as they hung downward toward the water, yet too weak to stand out and up to the passing breeze. The exquisite delicacy of these trembling little leaves, the arching elegance of the branches that had just opened them to the light, made it seem almost sacrilegious to turn the lens upon them.

Often since have I visited the same spot, in hope to see again this awakening, but without avail. The leaves show me their silky completeness, rustling above the stream in softest tree talk; the curious staminate flower-clusters hang like bunches of inverted commas; the neat little burs, with their inoffensive prickles, mature and discharge the angular nuts--but I am not again, I fear, to be present at the hour of the leaf-birth of the beech's year.

The beech, by the way, is tenacious of its handsome foliage. Long after most trees have yielded their leaves to the frost, the beech keeps its clothing, turning from the clear yellow of fall to lightest fawn, and hanging out in the forest a sign of whiteness that is cheering in the winter and earliest spring. These bleached-out leaves will often remain until fairly pushed off by the opening buds of another year.

Of the hazelnut or filbert, I know nothing from the tree side, but I cannot avoid mentioning another botanically unrelated so-called hazel--the witch-hazel. This small tree is known to most of us only as giving name to a certain soothing extract. It is worthy of more attention, for its curious and delicately sweet yellow flowers, seemingly clusters of lemon-colored threads, are the very last to bloom, opening bravely in the very teeth of Jack Frost. They are a delight to find, on the late fall rambles; and the next season they are followed by the still more curious fruits, which have a habit of suddenly opening and fairly ejaculating their seeds. A plucked branch of these fruits, kept in a warm place a few hours, will show this--another of nature's efficient methods for spreading seeds, in full operation--if one watches closely enough. The flowers and the fruits are on the tree at the same time, just as with the orange of the tropics.

Speaking of a tropical fruit, I am reminded that the greatest nut of all, though certainly not an American native, is nevertheless now grown on American soil. Some years ago a grove of lofty cocoanut palms in Yucatan fascinated me, and the opportunity to drink the clear and refreshing milk (not milky at all, and utterly different from the familiar contents of the ripened nut of commerce) was gladly taken. Now the bearing trees are within the bounds of the United States proper, and the grand trees in Southern Florida give plenty of fruit. The African citizens of that neighborhood are well aware of the refreshing character of the "juice" of the green cocoanut, and a friend who sees things for me with a camera tells with glee how a "darky" at Palm Beach left him in his wheel-chair to run with simian feet up a sloping trunk, there to pull, break open, and absorb the contents of a nut, quite as a matter of course. I have myself seen the Africans of the Bahamas in the West Indies climbing the glorious cocoa palms of the coral keys, throwing down the mature nuts, and then, with strong teeth, stripping the tough outer covering to get at the refreshing interior.

All these nut trees are only members of the great family of trees given by God for man's good, I firmly believe; for man first comes into Biblical view in a garden of trees, and the city and the plain are but penances for sin!

Some Other Trees

In preceding chapters of this series I have treated of trees in a relationship of family, or according to some noted similarity. There are, however, some trees of my acquaintance of which the family connections are remote or unimportant, and there are some other trees of individual merit with the families of which I am not sufficiently well acquainted to speak familiarly as a whole. Yet many of these trees, looked at by themselves, are as beautiful, interesting, and altogether worthy as any of which I have written, and they are also among the familiar trees of America. Therefore I present a few of them apart from the class treatment.

* * * * *

One day in very early spring--or was it very late in winter?--I walked along the old canal road, looking for some evidence in tree growth that spring was really at hand. Buds were swelling, and here and there a brave robin could be heard telling about it in song to his mate (I think that settled the season as earliest spring!); but beyond the bud evidences the trees seemed to be silent on the subject. Various herbs showed lusty beginnings, and the skunk-cabbage, of course, had pushed up its tropical richness in defiance of any late frost, pointing the way to its peculiar red-purple flowers, long since fertilized and turning toward maturity.

The search seemed vain, until a glint of yellow just ahead, too deep to proceed from the spice-bush I was expecting to find, drew me to the very edge of the water, there to see hanging over and reflected in the stream a mass of golden catkins. Looking closely, and touching the little tree, I disengaged a cloud of pollen and a score of courageous bees, evidently much more pleased with the sweet birch than with the near-by skunk-cabbage flowers. Sweet birch it was; the stiff catkins, that had all winter held themselves in readiness, had just burst into bloom with the sun's first warmth, introducing a glint of bright color into the landscape, and starting the active double work of the bees, in fertilizing flowers while gathering honey, that was not to be intermitted for a single sunshine hour all through the season.

A little later, along the great Susquehanna, I found in full bloom other trees of this same birch, beloved of boys--and of girls--for its aromatic bark. Certainly picturesque and bright, the little trees were a delight to the winter-wearied eye, the mahogany twigs and the golden catkins, held at poise over the water, being full of spring suggestion.

All of the birches--I wish I knew them better!--are good to look at, and I think the bees, the woodpeckers, the humming-birds and other wood folk must find some of them good otherwise. At Eagles Mere there was a yellow birch in the bark of which scores of holes had been drilled by the woodpeckers or the bees, at regularly spaced intervals, to let the forest life drink at will of the sweet sap. I remember also that my attempt to photograph a score of bees, two large brown butterflies and one humming-bird, all in attendance upon this birch feast, was a surprising failure. I secured a picture of the holes in the bark, to be sure, but the rapidly moving insect and bird life was too quick for an exposure of even a fraction of a second, and my negative was lifeless. These same yellow birches, picturesque in form, ragged in light-colored bark, give a brightness all their own to the deep forest, mostly of trees with rather somber bark.

A woodsman told me one summer of the use of old birch bark for starting a fire in the wet woods, and I have since enjoyed collecting the bark from fallen trees in the forest. It strips easily, in large pieces, from decayed stems, and when thrown on an open fire, produces a cheery and beautiful blaze, as well as much heat; while, if cunningly handled, by its aid a fire can be kindled even in a heavy rain.

The great North Woods show us wonderful birches. Paddling through one of the Spectacle ponds, along the Racquette river, one early spring day, I came upon a combination of white pine, red pine, and paper-birch that was simply dazzling in effect. This birch has bark, as every one knows, of a shining creamy white. Not only its color, but its tenacity, resistance to decay, and wonderful divisibility, make this bark one of the most remarkable of nature's fabrics. To the Indian and the trapper it has long been as indispensable as is the palm to the native of the tropics.

There are other good native birches, and one foreigner--the true white birch--whose cut-leaved form, a familiar lawn tree of drooping habit, is worth watching and liking. The name some of the nurserymen have given it, of "nine-bark," is significantly accurate, for at least nine layers may be peeled from the glossy whiteness of the bark of a mature tree.

I intend to know more of the birches, and to see how the two kinds of flowers act to produce the little fruits, which are nuts, though they hardly look so. And I would urge my tree-loving friends to plant about their homes these cheery and most elegantly garbed trees.

The spice-bush, of which I spoke above, is really a large shrub, and is especially notable for two things--the way it begins the spring, and the way it ends the fall. About my home, it is the first of wild woods trees to bloom, except perhaps the silver maple, which has a way of getting through with its flowers unnoticed before spring is thought of. One finds the delicate little bright yellow flowers of the spice-bush clustered thickly along the twigs long before the leaves are ready to brave the chill air. After the leaves have fallen in the autumn, these flowers stand out in a reincarnation of scarlet and spicy berries, which masquerade continually as holly berries when cunningly introduced amid the foliage of the latter. Between spring and fall the spice-bush is apparently invisible.

How many of us, perfectly familiar with "the holly berry's glow" about Christmas time, have ever seen a whole tree of holly, set with berries? Yet the trees, sometimes fifty feet high, of American holly--and this is very different from the English holly in leaf--grow all along the Atlantic sea-board, from Maine to Florida, and are especially plenty south of Maryland and Delaware. There is one superb specimen in Trenton, New Jersey's capital, which is of the typical form, and when crowded with scarlet berries it is an object of great beauty. One reason why many of us have not seen holly growing in the wild is that it seems to prefer the roughest and most inaccessible locations. Years ago I was told that I might see plenty of holly growing freely in the Pennsylvania county of my home. "But," my informant added, "you will need to wear heavy leather trousers to get to it!" The nurserymen are removing this difficulty by growing plants of all the hollies--American, Japanese, English and Himalayan--so that they may easily be set in the home grounds, with their handsome evergreen foliage and their berries of red or black.

One spring, the season and my opportunities combined to provide a most pleasing feast of color in the tree quest. It was afforded by the juxtaposition at Conewago of the bloom-time of the deep pink red-bud, miscalled "Judas tree," and the large white dogwood,--both set against the deep, almost black green of the American cedar, or juniper. These two small trees, the red-bud and the dogwood, are of the class of admirable American natives that are notable rather for beauty and brightness of bloom than for tree form or size.

The common dogwood--Cornus florida of the botany--appears in bloom insidiously, one might say; for the so-called flowers open slowly, and they are green in color, and easily mistaken for leaves, after they have attained considerable size. Gradually the green pales to purest white, and the four broad bracts, with the peculiar little pucker at the end of each, swell out from the real flowers, which look like stamens, to a diameter of often four inches. With these flowers clustered thickly on the usually flat, straight branches, the effect against the green or brown of near-by trees is startling. The dogwood's horizontal branching habit makes every scrap of its lovely white blooms effective to the beholder on the ground below, but far more striking if one may see it from above, as looking down a hillside.

Though the dogwood blooms before its leaves are put forth, the foliage sometimes catches up with the flowers; and this foliage is itself a pleasure, because of its fineness and its regular venation, or marking with ribs. In the fall, when the flowers of purest white have been succeeded by oblong berries of brightest scarlet, the foliage remains awhile to contrast with the brilliance of the fruit. The frosts soon drop the leaves, and then the berries stand out in all their attractiveness, offering food to every passing bird, and thus carrying out another of nature's cunning provisions for the reproduction of the species. Seeds in the crops of birds travel free and far, and some fall on good ground!

Is it not sad to know that the brave, bold dogwood, holding out its spring flag of truce from arduous weather, and its autumn store of sustenance for our feathered friends, is in danger of extinction from the forest because its hardy, smooth, even-grained white wood has been found to be especially available in the "arts"? I feel like begging for the life of every dogwood, as too beautiful to be destroyed for any mere utility.

I have been wondering as to the reason for the naming of the cornuses as dogwoods, and find in Bailey's great Cyclopedia of Horticulture the definite statement that the name was attached to an English red-branched species because a decoction of the bark was used to wash mangy dogs! This is but another illustration of the inadequacy and inappropriateness of "common" names.

There are many good dogwoods--the Cornus family is admirable, both in its American and its foreign members--but I must not become encyclopedic in these sketches of just a few tree favorites. I will venture to mention one shrub dogwood--I never heard its common name, but it has three botanical names (Cornus sericea, or coerulea, or Amomum, the latter preferred) to make up for the lack. It ought to be called the blue-berried dogwood, by reason of its extremely beautiful fruit, which formed a singular and delightful contrast to the profusion of red and scarlet fruits so much in evidence, one September day, in Boston's berry-full Franklin Park.

The red-bud, as I have said, is miscalled Judas-tree, the tradition being that it was on a tree of this family, but not of the American branch, happily and obviously, that the faithless disciple hanged himself after his final interview with the priests who had played upon his cupidity. Indeed, tradition is able to tell even now marvelous stories to travelers, and not long ago I was more amused than edified to hear an eloquent clergyman just returned from abroad tell how he had been shown the fruits of the Judas-tree, "in form like beautiful apples, fair to the eye, but within bitter and disappointing;" and he moralized just as vigorously on this fable as if it had been true, as he thought it. He didn't particularly relish the suggestion that the pulpit ought to be fairly certain of its facts, whether of theology or of science, in these days; but he succumbed to the submission of authority for the statement that the Eastern so-called Judas-tree, Cercis siliquastrum, bore a small pod, like a bean, and was not unpleasant, any more than the pod was attractive.

I mention this only in reprobation of the unpleasant name that really hurts the estimation of one of the most desirable and beautiful of America's smaller trees. The American red-bud is a joy in the spring about dogwood time, for it is all bloom, and of a most striking color. Deep pink, or purplish light red, or clear bright magenta--all these color names fit it approximately only. One is conscious of a warm glow in looking toward the little trees, with every branch clear down to the main stem not only outlined but covered with richest color.

There is among the accompanying illustrations (page 201) a photograph of a small but characteristic red-bud in bloom, looking at which reminds me of one of the pleasantest experiences of my outdoor life. With a cameristic associate, I was in a favorite haunt, seeing dogwoods and red-buds and other things of spring beauty, when a sudden warm thunder shower overtook us. Somewhat protected in our carriage--and it would have been more fun if we had stood out to take the rain as comfortably as did the horse--we saw the wonder of the reception of a spring shower by the exuberant plant life we were there to enjoy. When the clouds suddenly obscured the sky, and the first drops began to fall, the soft new umbrellas of the May-apples, raised to shield the delicate white flowers hidden under them from the too ardent sunshine, reversed the usual method by closing tightly and smoothly over the blooms, thus protecting perfectly their pollen hearts, and offering little resistance to the sharp wind that brought the rain. At our very feet we could see the open petals of the spring beauty coil up into tight little spirals, the young leaves on the pin-oaks draw in toward the stems from which they had been expanding. Over the low fence, the blue phlox, that dainty carpeting of the May woods, shut its starry flowers, and lay close to the ground. Quiet as we were, we could see the birds find sheltered nooks in the trees about us.

But soon the rain ceased, the clouds passed away, and the sun shone again, giving us a rainbow promise on the passing drops. Everything woke up! The birds were first to rejoice, and a veritable oratorio of praise and joyfulness sounded about our ears. The leaves quickly expanded, fresher than ever; the flowers uncurled and unfolded, the May-apple umbrellas raised again; and all seemed singing a song as joyous as that of the birds, though audible only to the nerves of eye and brain of the human beings who had thus witnessed another of nature's interior entertainments.

How much we miss by reason of fear of a little wetting! Many of the finest pictures painted by the Master of all art are visible only in rain and in mist; and the subtlest coloring of tree leaf and tree stem is that seen only when the dust is all washed away by the shower that should have no terrors for those who care for the truths of nature. In these days of rain-proof clothing, seeing outdoors in the rain is not even attended by the slightest discomfort, and I have found my camera quite able to stand a shower!

Another of the early spring-flowering small trees--indeed, the earliest one that blooms in white--is the shad-bush, or service-berry. Again the "common" names are trifling and inadequate; shad-bush because the flowers come when the shad are ascending the rivers along which the trees grow, and service-berry because the pleasant fruits are of service, perhaps! June-berry, another name, is better; but the genus owns the mellifluous name of Amelanchier, and the term Canadensis belongs to the species with the clouds of little white flowers shaped like a thin-petaled star. The shad-bush blooms with the trilliums--but I may not allow the spring flowers to set me spinning on another hank!

Searching for early recollections of trees, I remember, when a boy of six or seven, finding some little green berries or fruits, each with its long stem, on the pavement under some great trees in the Capitol Park of my home town. I could eat these; and thus they pleased the boy as much as the honey-sweet flowers that gave rise to them now please the man. The noble American linden, one of the really great trees of our forests, bears these delicate whitish flowers, held in rich clusters from a single stem which is attached for part of its length to a curious long green bract. If these flowers came naked on the tree, as do those of the Norway maple, for instance, they would be easily seen and admired of men, but being withheld until the splendid heart-shaped foliage is well out, the blooms miss the casual eye. But the bees see them; they know the linden for their own, and great stores of sweetest honey follow a year when abundant pasture of these flowers is available.

A kindly tree is this linden, or lime, or basswood, to give it all its common names. Kindly as well as stately, but never rugged as the oak, or of obvious pliant strength as the hickory. The old tree invites to shade under its limbs crowded with broad leaves; the young tree is lusty of growth and clean of bark, a model of rounded beauty and a fine variant from the overworked maples of our streets.

Again, the tale of woe! for the great lindens of our forests are nearly all gone. Too useful for timber; too easy to fell; its soft, smooth, even wood too adaptable to many uses! Cut them all; strip the bark for "bast," or tying material; America is widening; the sawmills cannot be idle; scientific and decent forestry, so successful and so usual in Europe, is yet but a dream for future generations here in America!

But other lindens, those of Europe especially, are loved of the landscape architect and the Germans. "Unter den Linden," Berlin's famous street, owes its name, fame and shade to the handsome European species, the white-lined leaves of which turn up in the faintest breeze, to show silvery against the deep green of their upper surfaces. Very many of these fine lindens are being planted now in America by landscape architects, and there are some lindens on Long Island just as prim and trim as any in Berlin. Indeed, there is a sort of German "offiziere" waxed-mustache air of superiority about them, anyway!

There is an all-pervading Middle States tree that I might give a common name to as the "fence-post tree," because it is so often grown for that use only, by reason of its enduring timber and its exceeding vigor under hard usage. Yet the common black locust is one of the most distinct and pleasing American trees of moderate height. Distinct it is in its framework in winter, mayhap with the twisted pods of last season's fruits hanging free; distinct again in its long-delayed late-coming acacia-like foliage; but fragrant, elegant and beautiful, as well as distinct, when in June it sets forth its long, drooping racemes of whitest and sweetest flowers. These come only when warm weather is an assured fact, and the wise Pennsylvania Germans feel justified in awaiting the blooming of the locust before finally discarding their winter underclothing!

For years a family of my knowledge has held it necessary, for its proper conduct, to have in order certain floral drives. First the apple blossom drive introduces the spring, and the lilac drive confirms the impression that really the season is advancing; but the locust drive is the sweetest of all, taking these nature lovers along some shady lanes, beside the east bank of a great river, and in places where, the trees planted only for the fence utility of the hard yellow wood, these fragrant flowers, hanging in grace and elegance far above the highway, have redeemed surroundings otherwise sordid and mean.

I want Americans to prize the American locust for its real beauty. The French know it, and show with pride their trifling imported specimens. We cannot exterminate the trees, and there will be plenty for posts, too; but let us realize its sweetness and elegance, as well as the durability of its structure.

There are fashions in trees, if you please, and the nurserymen set them. Suddenly they discover the merits of some long-forgotten tree, and it jumps into prominence. Thus, only a few years ago, the pin-oak came into vogue, to the lasting benefit of some parks, avenues and home grounds. Then followed the sycamore, but it had to be the European variety, for our own native "plane tree," or "button-ball," is too plentiful and easy to sing much of a tree-seller's song about. This Oriental plane is a fine tree, however, and the avenue in Fairmount Park that one may see from trains passing over the Schuylkill river is admirable. The bark is mottled in green, and especially bright when wet with rain. As the species is free from the attacks of a nasty European "bug," or fungus, which is bothering the American plane, it is much safer to handle, commercially.

But our stately American sycamore is in a different class. One never thinks of it as a lawn tree, or as bordering a fashionable roadway; rather the expectation is to find it along a brook, in a meadow, or in some rather wild and unkempt spot. As one of the scientific books begins of it, "it is a tree of the first magnitude." I like that expression; for the sycamore gives an impression of magnitude and breadth; it spreads out serenely and comfortably.

My friend Professor Bailey says Platanus occidentalis, which is the truly right name of this tree, has no title to the term sycamore; it is properly, as his Cyclopedia gives it, Buttonwood, or Plane. Hunting about a little among tree books, I find the reason for this, and that it explains another name I have never understood. The sycamore of the Bible, referred to frequently in the Old Testament, traditionally mentioned as the tree under which Joseph rested with Mary and the young child on the way to Egypt, and into which Zaccheus climbed to see what was going on, was a sort of fig tree--"Pharaoh's Fig," in fact. When the mystery-plays of the centuries gone by were produced in Europe, the tree most like to what these good people thought was the real sycamore furnished the branches used in the scene-setting--and it was either the oriental plane, or the sycamore-leaved maple that was chosen, as convenient. The name soon attached itself to the trees; and when homesick immigrants looked about the new world of America for some familiar tree, it was easy enough to see a great similarity in our buttonwood, which thus soon became sycamore.

So much for information, more or less legendary, I confess; but the great tree we are discussing is very tangible. Indeed, it is always in the public eye; for it carries on a sort of continuous disrobing performance! The snake sheds his skin rather privately, and comes forth in his new spring suit all at once; the oak and the maple, and all the rest of them continually but invisibly add new bark between the splitting or stretching ridges of the old; but our wholesome friend the sycamore is quite shamelessly open about it, dropping off a plate or a patch here and there as he grows and swells, to show us his underwear, which thus at once becomes overcoat, as he goes on. At first greenish, the under bark thus exposed becomes creamy white, mostly; and I have had a conceit that the colder the winter, the whiter would be those portions of Mr. Buttonball's pajamas he cared to expose to us the next spring!

The leaves of the sycamore are good to look at, and efficient against the sun. The color above is not as clear and sharp as that of the maple; underneath the leaves are whitish, and soft, or "pubescent," as the botanical term goes. Quite rakishly pointed are the tips, and the whole effect, in connection with the balls,--which are first crowded clusters of flowers, and then just as crowded clusters of seeds--is that of a gentleman of the old school, dignified in his knee-breeches and cocked hat, fully aware that he is of comfortable importance!

Those little button-balls that give name to this good American tree follow the flower clusters without much change of form--they were flowers, they are seeds--and they stay by the tree persistently all winter, blowing about in the sharp winds. After a while one is banged often enough to open its structure, and then the carrying wind takes on its wings the neat little cone-shaped seeds, each possessed of its own silky hairs to help float it gently toward the ground--and thus is another of nature's curious rounds of distribution completed.

A tree is never without interest to those whose eyes have been opened to some of the wonders and perfections of nature. Nevertheless, there is a time in the year's round when each tree makes its special appeal. It may be in the winter, when every twig is outlined sharply against the cold sky, and the snow reflects light into the innermost crevices of its structure, that the elm is most admirable. When the dogwood has on its white robe in May and June, it then sings its song of the year. The laden apple tree has a pure glory of the blossoms, and another warmer, riper glory of the burden of fruit, but we think most kindly of its flowering time. Some trees maintain such a continuous show of interest and beauty that it is difficult to say on any day, "Now is this tulip or this oak at its very finest!" Again, the spring redness of the swamp maple is hardly less vivid than its mature coloring of the fall.

But as to the liquidambar, or sweet-gum, there can be no question. Interesting and elegant the year round, its autumn covering of polished deep crimson starry leaves is so startlingly beautiful and distinct as to almost take it out of comparison with any other tree. Others have nearly the richness of color, others again show nearly the elegance of leaf form, but no one tree rivals completely the sweet-gum at the time when the autumn chill has driven out all the paleness in its leaf spectrum, leaving only the warm crimson that seems for awhile to defy further attacks of frost.

As to shape, the locality settles that; for, a very symmetrical small to maximum-sized tree in the North and on high dry places, in the South and in wet places north it becomes another "tree of the first magnitude," wide-spreading and heavy. A stellar comparison seems to fit, because of these wonderful leaves. They struck me at first, hunting photographs one day, as some sort of a maple; but what maple could have such perfection of star form? A maple refined, perfected, and indeed polished, one might well think, for while other trees have shining leaves, they are dull in comparison with the deep-textured gloss of these of the sweet-gum.

Here, too, is a tree for many places; an adaptable, cosmopolitan sort of arboreal growth. At its full strength of hard, solid, time-defying wooded body on the edge of some almost inaccessible swamp of the South, where its spread-out roots and ridgy branches earn for it another common name as the "alligator tree," it is in a park or along a private driveway at the North quite the acme of refined tree elegance, all the summer and fall. It takes on a rather narrow, pyramidal head, broadening as it ages, but never betraying kin with its fellow of the swamp, save perhaps when winter has bared its peculiar winged and strangely "corky" branches.

These odd branches bear, on some trees particularly, a noticeable ridge, made up of the same substance which in the cork-oak of Europe furnishes the bottle-stoppers of commerce. It makes the winter structure of the sweet-gum most distinct and picturesque, which appearance is accentuated by the interesting little seed-balls, or fruits, rounded and spiny, that hang long from the twigs. These fruits follow quickly an inconspicuous flower that in April or May has made its brief appearance, and they add greatly to the general attractiveness of the tree on the lawn, to my mind. Years ago I first made acquaintance with the liquidambar, as it ought always to be called, one wet September day, when an old tree-lover took me out on his lawn to see the rain accentuate the polish on the starry leaves and drip from the little many-pointed balls. I found that day that a camera would work quite well under an umbrella, and I obtained also a mind-negative that will last, I believe, as long as I can think of trees.

The next experience was in another state, where a quaint character, visited on business, struck hands with me on tree-love, and took me to see his pet liquidambar at the edge of a mill-pond. That one was taller, and quite stately; it made an impression, deepened again when the third special showing came, this time on a college campus, the young tree being naked and corky, and displayed with pride by the college professor who had gotten out of his books into real life for a joyous half day.

He wasn't the botany professor, if you please; that dry-as-dust gentleman told me, when I inquired as to what I might find in early bloom, or see with the eyes of an ignorant plant-lover, that there was "nothing blooming, and nothing of interest." He added that he had a fine herbarium where I might see all the plants I wanted, nicely dried and spread out with pins and pasters, their roots and all!

Look at dead plants, their roots indecently exposed to mere curiosity, on a bright, living early April day? Not much! I told my trouble to the professor of agriculture, whose eyes brightened, as he informed me he had no classes for that morning, and--"We would see!" We did see a whole host of living things outdoors,--flowers peeping out; leaves of the willows, just breaking; buds ready to burst; all nature waiting for the sun's call of the "grand entree." It was a good day; but I pitied that poor old dull-eyed herbarium specimen of a botanical professor, in whose veins the blood was congealing, when everything about called on him to get out under the rays of God's sun, and study, book in hand if he wanted, the bursting, hurrying facts of the imminent spring.

But a word more about the liquidambar--the name by which I hope the tree we are discussing may be talked of and thought of. Old Linn 鶀 s gave it that name, because it described euphoniously as well as scientifically the fact that the sap which exudes from this fine American tree is liquid amber. Now isn't that better than "gum" tree?

With trees in general as objects of interest, I have always felt a special leaning toward tropical trees, probably because they were rare, and indeed not to be seen outside of the conservatory in our Middle States. My first visit to Florida was made particularly enjoyable by reason of the palms and bananas there to be seen, and I have by no means lost the feeling of admiration for the latter especially. In Yucatan there were to be seen other and stranger growths and fruits, and the novelty of a great cocoanut grove is yet a memory not eclipsed by the present-day Floridian and Bahamian productions of the same sort.

It was, therefore, with some astonishment that I came to know, a few years ago, more of a little tree bearing a fruit that had been familiar from my boyhood, but which I was then informed was the sole northern representative of a great family of tropical fruits, and which was fairly called the American banana. The papaw it was; a fruit all too luscious and sweet, when fully ripe in the fall, for most tastes, but appealing strongly to the omnivorous small boy. I suppose most of my readers know its banana-like fruits, four or five inches long, green outside, but filled with soft and sweet aromatic yellow pulp, punctuated by several fat bean-like seeds.

But it is the very handsome and distinct little tree, with its decidedly odd flowers, I would celebrate, rather than the fruits. This tree, rather common to shady places in eastern America as far north as New York, is worth much attention, and worth planting for its spreading richness of foliage. The leaves are large, and seem to carry into the cold North a hint of warmth and of luxuriant growth not common, by any means--I know of only one other hardy tree, the cucumber magnolia, with an approaching character. The arrangement of these handsome papaw leaves on the branches, too, makes the complete mass of regularly shaped greenery that is the special characteristic of this escape from the tropics; and, since I have seen the real papaw of the West Indies in full glory, I am more than ever glad for the handsomer tree that belongs to the regions of cold and vigor.

The form of our papaw, or Asimina triloba--the botanical name is rather pleasing--is noticeable, and as characteristic as its leafage. See these side branches, leaving the slender central stem with a graceful up-curve, but almost at once swinging down, only to again curve upward at the ends! Are they not graceful? Such branches as these point nature's marvelous engineering, to appreciate which one needs only to try to imagine a structure of equal grace and efficiency, made with any material of the arts. How awkward and clumsy steel would be, or other metal!

Along these swinging curved branches, as we see them in the April winds, there appear hints of the leaf richness that is to come--but something else as well. These darkest purple-red petals, almost black, as they change from the green of their opening hue, make up the peculiar flowers of the papaw. There is gold in the heart of the flower, not hid from the bees, and there is much of interest for the seeker for spring knowledge as well; though I advise him not to smell the flowers. Almost the exact antithesis of the dogwood is the bloom of this tree; for, both starting green when first unfolded from the buds, the papaw's flowers advance through browns and yellows, dully mingled, to the deep vinous red of maturity. The dogwood's final banner of white is unfolded through its progress of greens, about the same time or a little later.

A pleasant and peculiar small tree is this papaw, not nearly so well known or so highly esteemed as it ought to be.

Another tree with edible fruits--but here there will be a dispute, perhaps!--is the persimmon. I mean the American persimmon, indissolubly associated in our own Southland with the darky and the 'possum, but also well distributed over Eastern North America as far north as Connecticut. The botanical name of the genus is Diospyros, liberally translated as "fruit of the gods," or "Jove's fruit." If his highness of Olympus was, by any chance, well acquainted with our 'simmon just before frost, he must have had a copper-lined mouth, to choose it as his peculiar fruit!

Making a moderate-sized tree of peculiar and pleasing form, its branches twisting regardless of symmetry, the persimmon in Pennsylvania likes the country roadsides, especially along loamy banks. Here it has unequaled opportunity for hanging out its attractively colored fruits. As one drives along in early fall, just before hard frost, these fine-looking little tomato-like globes of orange and red are advertised in the wind by the absence of the early dropping foliage. They look luscious and tempting; indeed, they are tempting! Past experience--you need but one--had prepared me for this "bunko" fruit; but my friend would not believe me, one day in early October--he must taste for himself. Taste he did, and generously, for the first bite is pleasing, and does not alarm, wherefore he had time, before his insulted nerves of mouth and tongue gave full warning, to absorb two of the 'simmons. Whew! What a face he made when the puckering juice got to work, and convinced him that he had been sucking a disguised lump of alum. Choking and gasping, he called for the water we were far from; and he won't try an unfrosted persimmon again!

My clerical friend who brought home the fairy tale about the red-bud, or Judas-tree, might well have based his story on the American persimmon, but for the fact that this puckery little globe, so brilliant and so deceptive before frost, loses both its beauty and its astringency when slightly frozen. Then its tender flesh is suave and delicious, and old Jove might well choose it for his own.

But the tree--that is a beauty all summer, with its shining leaves, oblong, pointed and almost of the magnolia shape. It will grace any situation, and is particularly one of the trees worth planting along highways, to relieve the monotony of too many maples, ashes, horse-chestnuts and the like, and to offer to the passer-by a tempting fruit of which he will surely not partake too freely when it is most attractive. I read that toward the Western limit of its range the persimmon, in Louisiana, Eastern Kansas and the Indian Territory, becomes another tree of the first magnitude, towering above a hundred feet. This would be well worth seeing!

There is another persimmon in the South, introduced from Japan, the fruits of which are sold on the fruit-stands of Philadelphia, Boston and New York. This, the "kaki" of Japan, is a small but business-like tree, not substantially hardy north of Georgia, which provides great quantities of its beautiful fruits, rich in coloring and sweet to the taste, and varying greatly in size and form in its different varieties. These 'simmons do not need the touch of frost, nor do they ever attain the fine, wild, high flavor of the frost-bitten Virginian fruits; the tree that bears them has none of the irregular beauty of our native persimmon, nor does it approach in size to that ornament of the countryside.

* * * * *

And now, in closing these sketches, I become most keenly sensible of their deficiencies. Purely random bits they are, coming from a busy man, and possessing the one merit of frankness. Deeply interested in trees, but lacking the time for continuous study, I have been turning my camera and my eyes upon the growths about me, asking questions, mentally recording what I could see, and, while thankful for the rest and the pleasure of the pursuit, always sorry not to go more fully into proper and scientific tree knowledge.

At times my lack in this respect has made me ashamed to have written at all upon trees; but with full gratitude to the botanical explorers whose labors have made such superficial observations as mine possible, I venture to send forth these sketches, without pretension as to the statement of any new facts or features.

  If anything I have here set down shall induce among those who have looked and read with me from nature's open book the desire to go more deeply into the fascinating tree lore that always awaits and inevitably rewards the effort, I shall cry heartily, "God-speed!"

###